101

Creative Programs
for Children

Jared R. Knight

Disclaimer
Every effort was made to provide safe children's programs with recommendations for age-appropriate activities, adult supervision, proper adult training and certification, suitable use of equipment, and suggested activity set-up requirements. The author and publisher specifically disclaim any liability arising from the use of any information in this book.

ISBN-13: 978-158518-010-3
ISBN-10: 1-58518-010-6
Library of Congress Control Number: 2006939032
Cover design: Studio J Art & Design
Book layout: Studio J Art & Design

Healthy Learning
P.O. Box 1828
Monterey, CA 93942
www.healthylearning.com

Dedication

Dedicated to the Memory of Wilma P. Knight

Acknowledgments

I would like to thank Glen and Bev Parker and Mark Longhurst at Aspen Grove Family Camp for their leadership and inspiration and for mentoring me in family camp programming. Special thanks to my wife, LaDonna, who provided insights and encouragement. I would like to thank Daniel Green at Healthy Learning for his guidance. I also would like to thank Holly Linford, Ben Jenkins, and Catherine Bridges for their assistance with this book. Lastly, thanks to my children, Rachel, Alex, and Emerson Knight, who provided the motivation to complete this project.

Foreword

Children of all ages thrive on programs that are action-oriented. Programs need to be challenging to the mind as the child grows and develops. They must be challenging to the young physical body as the child grows to adulthood. Keeping all programs appropriate for the child at a specific age or development brings satisfaction to the child and success to the program. If any program is too easy, interest will be lost. If too hard, the child won't participate. The wise leader selects and adapts the "just right" program for each occasion.

Programs that are new, first-time experiences for the child are exciting and adventurous if the child understands what is expected and how to participate. Each time the child has success with a new, first-time experience and enjoys it, the child will want to repeat the experience. First-time experiences, enjoyed and repeated, become fun times for the child. To be successful in the eyes of the children, all programs must be either adventurous or fun.

In his book, *101 Creative Programs for Children*, author Jared Knight shares his life of experience in providing programs for children. He shares 101 creative programs in 11 areas of interest, adventure, and fun. These programs fit a variety of situations, and the informed adult will never want for ideas for the next group activity. Programs in this book form an outstanding collection for:

- Summer camps (private, church, youth agency, or community)
- Community recreation programs for children
- School classrooms and fieldtrips
- Church children and youth groups
- Children and youth groups (e.g., Cub Scouts, Boy Scouts, Boys and Girls Clubs, Girl Scouts, YMCA, YWCA, 4-H Clubs)
- Families (family home evenings, family trips, family reunions)

Use of this book will not only provide immediate ideas for working with children, but will stimulate adult leaders to think of many others they will want to use. Good luck as you find success in working with children as they grow into responsible adults and good citizens of our communities and nation!

—Rulon Dean Skinner
Retired director of the Youth Leadership Program at Brigham Young University

Contents

Preface

This book was written as an autobiography, not because I am mentioned in any of the programs, but in the sense that all of the programs included in this book have been a part of my life. I speak firsthand of the benefit that these activities will have in the lives of children, teenagers, and young adults, because I have seen the positive impact from these programs in my own experience. I realize that many variations and other ways of implementing these games and crafts exist, but I have included as many activities as possible in the hope that they will enhance and strengthen any recreational or educational curriculum.

Introduction

These programs are designed for the development of children, including physical skills, cognitive exploration, social interaction, and character development. This book provides programs that will expand a child's vision of who he or she is, allowing him or her to be part of a team while being mentored by adult leadership.

The key ingredient for creative programming for children that will foster the imagination and capture learning is the establishment of a sense of wonder. Several program elements will assist in creating a fun environment where participants can learn and explore the many areas of child development. These program elements include games, music, treats, decorations, costumes, and crafts, and are included in the program design in each chapter of this book.

Adults should assume the largest role in creating a sense of wonder. In addition to providing a safe and organized program, adults should interact, play, and pretend with the children as the program is being implemented. The adult leaders who prepare these activities will lose the opportunity to mentor and rejuvenate themselves through the power of recreation and play if they sit back and watch the programs from afar. When youth leaders who need the leadership experience are involved, adults may need to delegate responsibilities and accountability, but they should still support and interact with each child.

The activities in this book can accommodate large or small groups of children. If the size of the group is larger than eight people, leaders can create smaller teams of children. You can also form teams of children out of a larger group so that the two teams can complete against each other. Based on the needs of each group, adult leaders can adjust the activities to be appropriate for children age four to 18. The tools and equipment needed for each program are listed for each activity.

Adult supervision should be a part of each activity, because many activities include the use of items such as marbles, beads, and latex balloons that are potential choking hazards. Adult leaders should ask parents about any food or latex allergies prior to the activities.

1

Building Confidence and Self-Worth

Program #1: Making a Friend

Breaking the Ice and Getting to Know You

Pass out the following questionnaire to a group of children. Have a race to see who can get a different signature for each of the questions the fastest. If no one in the group qualifies for a question, an adult leader can tell children to write the word "free" in the blank, indicating that they don't need to answer that question.

1. Owns a skateboard
2. Favorite color is blue
3. Was born the same month as you
4. Plays a musical instrument
5. Name starts with the same letter as yours
6. Has traveled to another country
7. Likes country music
8. Has a yellow toothbrush
9. Has two sisters
10. Has a pet cat

Tennis Ball Toss

Have the group form a circle in which the participants are standing shoulder-to-shoulder and facing the inside of the circle. Everyone introduces himself by stating his first name. After everyone has had a chance to state his name once, someone in the group throws a tennis ball to another participant. As the ball is being thrown, the thrower says the first name of the person he is throwing the tennis ball to. When the receiver gets the ball, he throws the ball to someone else in the circle. Each time the ball is caught, the receiver raises one hand in the air to indicate that he has received the ball and cannot catch it again. This way, everyone in the group will have an opportunity to catch the ball. After completing the first round, the group should repeat this activity in the same order, while the adult leader times the event and asks the children to increase the speed of completing the task. After the second round, the adult leader asks if it can be done faster. Eventually, the group should decide to tighten the circle to increase the speed. The fastest way to complete the round is to organize the group in a circle in the order that the children receive the ball. The hand of each participant is placed in the center of the circle and the ball rolls on each participant's hand as the children state the name of the person to whom they normally throw the ball. The ball quickly makes its way around the circle in the same order as in previous rounds.

High-Five

Have the children pair up and introduce themselves to each other by their first names. After learning each other's name, each child gives the other person five "high-fives" while saying his name. For the next round, everyone finds a new partner and, after introducing themselves, gives each other five "high-10s" using both hands while repeating each other's first name. For the third round, each child must find a new partner and, after the introductions, give each other a "high-15," which entails adding a foot to the "high-10." Each participant holds one leg out while the other person slaps his foot five times, repeating his name. For the last round—a "high-30"—the participants form groups of three, introduce themselves, and form a circle. Each child gives the person on his left a "high-five" while repeating his name. He then turns to the person on the right and slaps his foot five times while saying his name at the same time. With all four rounds completed, the participants find the first person they gave a "high-five" to and repeat the process, moving on to the people they greeted earlier in the same order.

Blanket Drop

Divide the group into two teams. Two leaders stand on chairs holding up a blanket to separate the two teams so that they cannot see each other. Each team chooses a participant to stand next to the blanket. The leaders drop the blanket and the object is for the participant to say his opponent's name. The participant who says the name last joins the other team. Play the game until one team takes all of the players.

Things in Common

Divide the group into smaller teams and have each team come up with 25 things they have in common. Children should be encouraged to think of items that are not obvious. For example, children should not just mention that the group is all wearing socks. Suggested items include attending a popular vacation site, having a certain number of brothers and sisters, having the letter "G" in their last names, and enjoying playing shuffleboard. After the team has come up with a list, have them make a name and a cheer for their team that lists many of the items they have in common.

What You Have Done

Everyone sits down in a large circle of chairs, with one less chair than participants. The person without a chair is "it." He stands in the middle of the circle and states that he has either done something or been somewhere. For example, "I have been to Jackson Hole, Wyoming." Everyone who has done that same thing has to leave his chair and find a vacant one. A variation to this game is the "I Have Never Done" game, in which the participants state something they have never done. For example, "I have never been to a Chinese restaurant." The people who have done that thing need to find a new chair.

Two Truths and One Lie

Each person in the group comes up with two truths and one lie about himself. Everyone else needs to guess which one is the lie.

Setting Goals

Have the team stand on a tarp. With markers in hand, have them write down their expectations for the team on the tarp. While they are still standing on the tarp, have them flip it over. Each individual needs to keep both feet on the tarp as the group turns it over. This feat is accomplished by having everyone in the group shuffle their feet to one corner of the tarp. Then, one participant in the group pulls another corner of the tarp over as the group steps on the new side of the tarp. The corner that the group previously was standing on is then turned over. Once the tarp is turned, have them write goals on the new side of the tarp. The expectations and goals can be individual or team oriented.

Processing

Ask each child how he felt at the beginning of the activity and how he feels once it's completed. Ask how he felt when he found out something he has in common with someone else in the group. Test someone's knowledge by having him name all of the participants.

Program #2: Team Building

Billboard

Give everyone half a sheet of cardstock with the following items printed on it:
- Name:
- Favorite food:
- Last vacation:
- Hobby:
- One word that describes you:

Use a string to hang the sign around the neck of each participant. During the course of the day, everyone on the team can learn about the interests of their teammates.

Names and Cheer

Each team should make up a name and cheer that it will use for other activities.

All Aboard

Divide the group into teams of 10 participants. Then, have everyone on the team stand at least one foot on a garbage can lid that is placed on the ground. When everyone is successfully balanced on the lid, have the team sing "Mary Had a Little Lamb" three times.

Human Knot

Have the children stand in a circle facing each other. Have them reach out with one arm and grab someone else's hand. With the other arm, they should reach out and grab a different person's hand. The circle of people should become a big knot. The group then needs to try to untangle the human knot. For safety, and to avoid twisting arms, the participants should rotate their wrists when moving around.

Community Culture

Have one participant leave the group while everyone else thinks of three behaviors that they are going to adopt when the participant comes back. The more subtle the better, so it is harder to figure out what the group has in common. For example, when someone in the group coughs, everyone else crosses their legs and claps their hands. The objective is to figure out what the group has or does that is common to everyone. The activity illustrates that no one should feel left out on a team.

Feel-Good Frisbee™

The participants stand in a circle. Each child tosses a Frisbee to someone else while stating something that he likes about that person. Adult leaders should make sure that everyone has a turn and receives a compliment.

Golf Ball Shoot

Cut two-inch PVC pipes in half and in two-foot lengths. Make sure you have enough for each participant to have a piece of pipe. Participants stand in a straight line facing one direction. Have them hold the PVC pipe out in front of them at approximately waist-level. The PVC pipes cannot touch each other and the participants cannot move around. An adult leader stands on one end of the line and drops tennis balls, golf balls, or marbles at the front of the line. The team tries to get all of the balls into a basket at the other end of the line without dropping any of the balls. If a ball drops, the team should run 10 feet away and yell "Kaboom" 10 times before running back and starting all over again.

T-Shirt or Bandanna

Having a common T-shirt differentiates the team from others and builds a strong sense of team identity. Colored bandannas are an inexpensive way to keep teams separated from a larger group.

Where in the Circle Am I?

Have the group stand in a circle and then have everyone in the group look quickly around to see who is standing by them. Blindfold all participants and have them get back into the circle in the same order that they started in without talking.

Blind Shapes

Have the participants form a circle, then blindfold them and have them make a square, triangle, and star. Another way to play this game is to blindfold everyone but one person. This person stands in the center of the circle and can see but cannot talk. The participants around the circle are blindfolded but can talk. This situation forces the group to communicate differently with each other as they design the shapes.

Trust Circle

Have the group form a tight circle with their hands out in front. One person stands in the middle, with his arms crossed against his chest, gently falls up against a person in the circle, and is then gently pushed to another person in the circle.

Processing

As the team develops, ask questions about the leader in each activity. Did the leader change with each game or was it the same person? How did each person contribute to accomplish the given task? Who became frustrated and why? What other ways did the group communicate when no one could talk?

Program #3: Dividing the Group Into Teams

These games should foster better team spirit and a sense of unity rather than a feeling of choosing sides. This random order of selecting teams will allow more interaction and allow the children to make new friends. When left to choose by themselves, children will pick a team with people they already know, thereby not allowing the opportunity to meet new people. The method of having team captains and choosing teams based upon skill or popularity will leave some children feeling left out. Teams should only be divided by children when the team captains value each player.

Mingle

Instruct the group to wander through the crowd while repeatedly saying "mingle." An adult leader then yells out, "Get into groups of _____." The leader can begin with larger-sized groups and work down to the desired size for the next activity.

Train Game

One person starts out acting as a train, chugging along in a middle of a circle of people. That individual comes up to a person and asks him his name. He then asks if he would like to join the train. The second person gets behind the first person and puts his hands on the shoulders of the leader. If the second person's name is Alex, then both people start chugging across the room chanting "Alex, Alex, Alex, Alex, Alex," until they come to another person. They will repeat the procedure, chanting the name of the third person. Eventually, a long line of people will be weaving through the room chanting each new passenger's name. Have several trains going at the same time, and have each train form a new group for the next activity.

Red Rover Red Rover

Two lines of people hold hands and face each other. They take turns calling for an individual to come over to their side. The individual tries to break through the chain on the opposing side. If that individual succeeds in breaking through, then that participant takes another participant back to his team. If he doesn't succeed in breaking through, then the team calls for a new person from the opposing team to break through their chain by saying, "Red rover red rover send (they choose a person's name) right over." This game brings two teams back into one big group, as one of the teams will eventually "win" everyone to its side.

Program #4: Designing and Learning About Flags

By designing a flag, teams of children establish a sense of unity and belonging. Everyone in the world is organized into groups that have a flag that bears their identity: countries, states, counties, cities, military units, churches, businesses, schools, youth groups, etc. The following activities will allow children to make their own team flag and learn about the importance of flags in their lives.

Team Flag

With fabric, glue, acrylic paint, felt, fabric markers, and a one-inch PVC pipe for the pole, children can design a fun flag. Flags can have themes. They can represent each team member, state goals or mission statements, or just be plain silly. Ribbons, patches, or items tied with string can be displayed on the team's flag in recognition of certain accomplishments achieved during other activities.

Individual Coat of Arms

Children can research their own family's coat of arms, or they can invent their own coat of arms. Adult leaders can teach about character, honesty, civility, and kindness, and have children paint a symbol or animal to represent each of these values.

Learning Different Countries and States Flags

Children can make coloring pages of different countries, providences, or states to learn and appreciate different flags. Also, they can learn the proper etiquette for displaying the United States flag, such as where to place it next to a speaker and how to display it outdoors or with another country or state flag.

Nautical Flags

Give children the opportunity to communicate with nautical flags. Each nautical flag represents a letter, number, or short phrase that enables passing ships to communicate with each other. Two-letter signals are also used. For example, AC means "I am abandoning my vessel" and QU means "anchoring is prohibited."

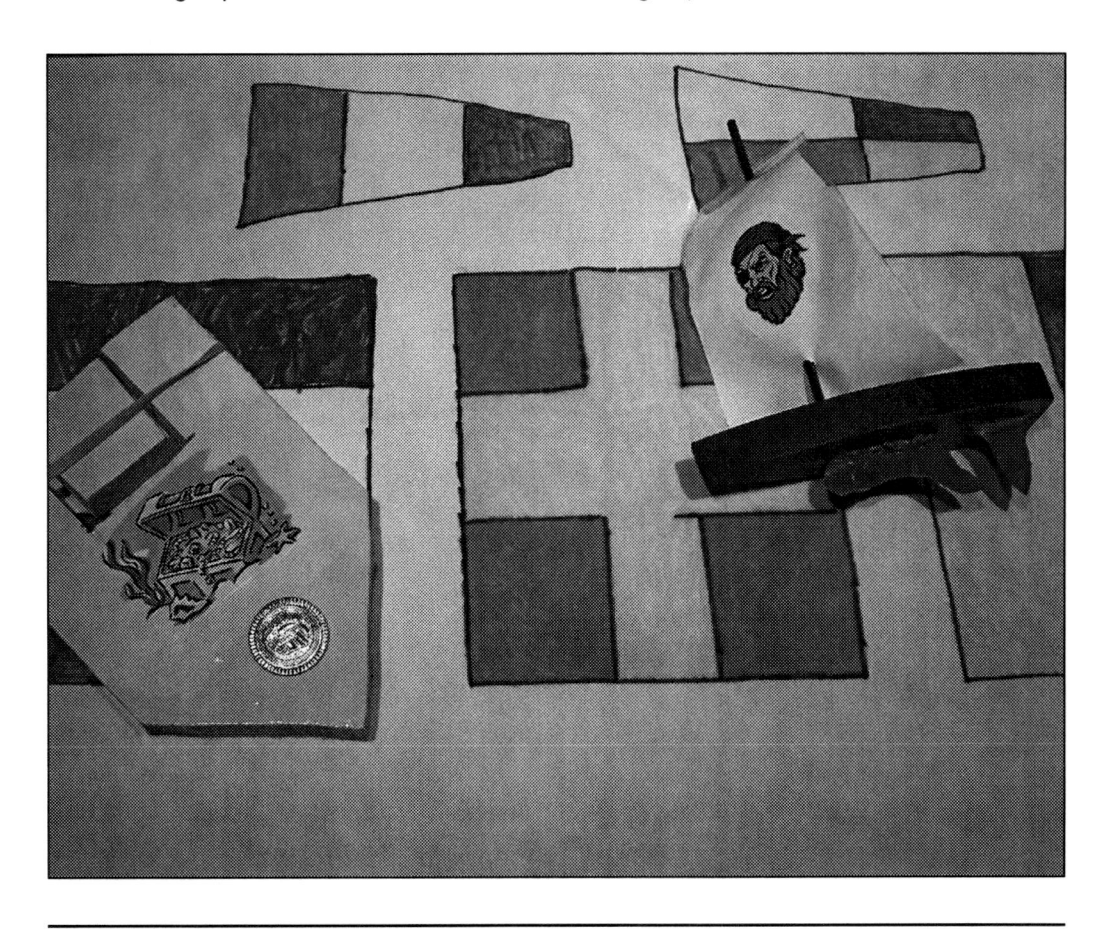

Learn to Communicate With the Semaphore Flag Signaling System

The semaphore flag signaling system is based on waving hand-held flags in a systematic order to communicate with another person at long distances. Semaphore flags are usually square. They are red and yellow, divided diagonally with red in the upper portion. One flag is held in each hand. Children can make these flags and try to communicate with each other. Hand positions determine a letter or number based on a clock pattern.

Capture the Flag

Divide a large field in half. At the end of each side, designate a "jail" and an area where the team's flag could be displayed. Each team tries to take the other's flag without getting caught. If a player is caught, he is sent to jail and can be rescued by a teammate, with free "walk-backs" to their side of the field.

2

Strengthening Imagination and Creativity

Program #5: King Arthur's Festival

A large castle sets the stage for this program. An inflatable castle can be rented through many party-supply stores. Children enjoy jumping up and down or they can play games inside the castle, such as trying to catch a ball before it bounces more than once.

Plywood Castle

Make a small square castle by joining sheets of plywood together with industrial-strength plastic ties. The plywood can be cut and painted to look like the outside of a castle. A small opening with a drawbridge at the front of the castle can be used as the entrance. The castle has no roof, so children can be supervised as they play. Put medieval toys, such as a plastic toy castle that includes action figures of kings, queens, knights, and dragons, inside the castle for them to play with.

Foam Sword Fighting

Children will enjoy the chance to learn techniques in sword fighting, using commercially purchased foam swords or foam swords made from a stick, duct tape, and heavy foam. Strict rules should be set in advance and children should wear ear and eye protection. Shields can be made out of heavy cardboard.

Jousting With Foam Noodles and Stick Horses

Children can gallop toward each other on stick horses using foam noodles in a medieval jousting contest. A small amount of washable tempera paint can be applied to the end of each noodle to determine who was hit first in the contest. Leaders may want to provide jousting participants with an oversized shirt so that children do not get too messy. Though the noodles are soft and flexible, each child should wear a plastic face shield in additional to eye and ear protection.

Jousting on Platforms

Two opposing participants each stand on a one-foot square wooden platform with a small, beveled triangular piece of wood attached to the bottom of the platform to make it wobbly. Each participant tries to knock off his opponent with foam-covered poles.

Friar Tuck and Little John's Log Push

A two-by-four piece of wood is used as a bridge. Two participants stand on the bridge and try to knock each other off using small "logs" made from rolled-up three-inch foam. The bridge should be secured to the ground with tent pegs.

Maypole

A maypole can either be purchased or made with an eight-foot pole, a wooden base, a round wooden top, and 10 long fabric streamers attached to the wooden top. Ten participants each hold the end of a streamer and braid them together by weaving in and out of the circle.

Robin Hood's Archery Tournament

A festive-looking archery tournament for children age 10 and older can be made by using large, round, hay-filled targets covered in burlap, recurve bows, and target cedar arrows. Rope off the archery area, and use certified and qualified archery leaders. Refer to Chapter 11, Program #89 for recommendations for setting up an archery range.

Riding Lawn Mower Dragon

With plywood, paint, and a lot of imagination, the children can convert a riding lawn mower into a dragon that can move around during the festival.

Puppet Show

Design a trifold puppet theater out of three half-sheets of plywood joined together with hinges. Cut a center stage out of the middle section and two smaller circles out of the

side sections. Cover the openings with fabric attached with a staple gun. Purchase medieval puppets such as wizards, dragons, and knights. Adults can read fairytales while children act them out with the puppets.

Costumes

Purchase medieval costumes for leaders and inexpensive foil crowns for participants. Have two leaders be a "king" and a "queen" and crown children with the foil crowns. Adult leaders can hold a ginger ale drinking contest from tankards.

Leprechaun's Gold Hunt

Children can make leprechaun houses out of cardboard milk cartons by cutting holes in the carton for the door and windows and applying construction paper with glue to form the walls and roof. Children then decorate the house with glitter by applying glue in creative patterns on the house and sprinkling the glue patterns with glitter. After the leprechaun house is completed, have the children hunt for candy, which is wrapped in gold foil and hidden in a plastic cauldron, by looking for a paper rainbow that is placed somewhere in the room.

Dragon's Tail

Give each participant a saltine cracker tied to a string that he can attach to his belt. Each participant has a rolled up newspaper he uses as a sword to swat the cracker off the string of the other participants. Each participant tries to keep the others from breaking his cracker "dragon's tail" off.

Program #6: Pirate Day

Sailboat Racing

Make a sailboat out of a piece of wood that is seven inches long, two inches wide, and one inch thick. Use a six-and-a-half-inch wooden dowel for the mast and make a sail out of a paper protector sheet that is two-and-a-half inches wide on the top and four inches wide at the bottom. Cut a small piece of plastic from a milk jug for a keel and rudder and have the children paint and design their boat. Set up two 10-foot-long rain gutters on two wooden sawhorses and fill them with water. Children race the vessels by blowing the sails of their boats.

Rubber Band Boat

Cut a one-inch-thick piece of wood in the shape of a boat, with a triangle cut at the bow (front) and a small square section cut out of the stern (rear). Twist a rubber band around a small piece of wood that is half the size of the cut-out section of the stern. Wrap both ends of the rubber band around the side of the stern. When the rubber band untwists, it will act as a propeller, thrusting the boat ahead.

Pirate Ship

An adult can cut a two-foot-long section of a two-by-four piece of wood and then router it. The adult must drill three holes for wooden dowels that will be the masts of the ship. Allow the children to sand and stain the ship and glue in the dowels. Hammer small nails into the masts and the bottom of the ship. Use three four-foot sections of colorful string to form the sails. The child starts with a string at the base of the ship and runs it to a nail at the top of the mast and back down to another nail at the base. After the

child does this several times on each of the different nails, the triangle pattern will form a sail. Each piece of string should be used for a different sail of the ship.

Treasure Hunt

Map out a pirate treasure using clues that will lead the children to a treasure chest of candy and plastic coins. Create a clever way to introduce the clues such as, "Arg, ye poor maties, there be a prize to be won. If you can outsmart the likes of me, Captain Red Beard, you could find yourself winning me hard-earned treasure. In order for ye to find me gold, ye must first follow me clues. There be four of them that will lead you." Make a map by hand or purchase treasure map paper at a party-supply store.

Geocaching

In this game, the children can find a treasure with a GPS receiver, using GPS coordinates posted on the Internet by people hiding the cache. Once the children find the cache, which is usually in a waterproof container, they must fill out the log book. Most importantly, they must return the cache to the exact position where it was found.

Dig for Buried Treasure With a Metal Detector

Take a group of children to a playground and have them find buried treasure with a metal detector. Each participant needs to wear leather gloves and use small plastic gardening trowels to dig out items. Many items may be rusty and should not be touched without gloves.

Costumes for Pirates

Add beards, mustaches, and face-paint scars to children who want to bear the looks of a salty old pirate. Have children make up their own pirate song. Use canning-jar lid rings with strings tied at the top for earrings that can hang around their ears. You can use paper towel rolls painted black as telescopes. Make paper hats out of black construction paper. You can make a pirate mask out of a paper plate and string, cutting out openings for the eyes, nose, and mouth. Let the children design the paper plate mask with markers and have them color the top of the mask to look like a bandanna.

Walk the Plank Relay

Each participant has a hoop (e.g., a Hula Hoop®) around his waist that represents his ship. When the relay starts, participants run toward cones placed 35 feet away and run back to the finish line, where the relay started. When Captain Red Beard yells "Walk the plank!" each participant must drop his hoop, run around it three times, put the hoop back on, and continue running toward the finish line. The winner of the relay is the first one to cross the finish line.

Program #7: Superhero Day

Make a cape for each child to wear during the superhero activities. Leaders should make sure that the cloth is not too tight around the child's neck and that it is not a tripping hazard.

Superhero Clay Model

With colored clay, pipe cleaners, and colored pieces of felt, the children make superheroes and invent a story in which the clay hero figure "saves the day."

Water Balloon Launch

Leaders throw water balloons high in the air and the children catch them with their superhero capes. The capes should not be attached to the child, but instead held out in front of the child with both hands.

Boulder Mover

A team of children needs to move a large exercise ball, which they pretend is a boulder, two feet off the ground for 50 feet without using their hands or feet.

Comic Book

Give each child a pad of paper, colored pencils, and a fine-tip marker and have him make a comic book starring himself. Have him create a plot, a villain, and a way that he, the hero, triumphs over evil. The themes to the stories can be from common, everyday situations or they can address more serious issues such as bullying, avoiding drugs, protecting against identify theft, or Internet stalking.

Creating Super Powers

Have children shoot a small rubber band off the end of their finger at a target. The target can be a half-sheet of plywood with five large holes cut out of it. In each hole, place an empty soda can hanging from string. Leaders need to make sure children wear eye protection.

Up, Up, and Away

This game gives children a sense of flying through the air while both feet are on the ground. Have children walk along a long piece of blue rope while looking through the wrong end of a pair of binoculars. They should pretend the rope is a river and put little cars and houses along the river. Depth perception becomes so distorted that the rope looks like it is 25 feet below and the toy cars look like they are 100 feet below. As the children walk on the rope, have them count how many times they step off the rope or step on cars and houses. The winner is the child who steps off the rope the fewest number of times and doesn't smash the village below.

Program #8: Monster Follies

Magic Show

Adults can perform magic tricks such as the magic coloring book that colors pages instantly, scarves that change colors, pulling a long string out of the magician's mouth, and various card and rope tricks. Most magic shops or websites have these tricks for sale. Teach children some basic magic tricks, like the taking off the thumb illusion and the ball and vase trick.

Thumb Trick—The thumb on the left hand should be bent back toward the magician to look like the top half of the thumb is missing. The thumb of the right hand should be bent and lined up with the left thumb to look like the top half of it. The fingers on the left hand should be straight out and the index finger of the right hand should cover where the right and left thumbs meet, so that the two thumbs look like one thumb. To remove the thumb, the magician moves the right thumb and index finger forward and leaves the left thumb bent, looking like a stub.

Ball and Vase Trick—The ball and vase trick can be purchased at a magic supply store. The trick is to have a small ball disappear and then reappear. To start, the magician shows a round ball to the audience. Two balls are used in this trick, but only one appears at a time to give the illusion that a single ball disappears and reappears. The first ball is a round ball that looks as if it is placed inside the three-inch plastic vase. The lid then covers the top of the vase. However, the round ball is not put in the vase, but instead, through sleight of hand, is placed in the magician's pocket. The second ball is attached to a false bottom in the vase. When the magician lifts the lid from the side, he lifts the false bottom with the lid, showing that the ball has disappeared. To make the ball come back, the magician lifts the top spire of the lid and the ball that is attached to the false bottom seems to appear back in the vase.

Spook Alley (Age 11 and Older)

To make this activity both fun and safe, the spook alley should *not* include any of the following items:
- Fake blood or severed fake body parts
- Mechanical power tools
- Monsters physically chasing participants
- Monsters touching participants
- Evil-looking masks

A spook alley should include suspense and anticipation, which can be achieved through music, lighting, glow-in-the-dark paint, black lights, fog, weird noises, and traditional monster masks. Fun masks include werewolves, vampires, mummies, witches, zombies, and mad scientists. Most children are familiar with these characters and might be temporarily frightened, but they shouldn't be too scared if the spook alley is done properly. Never blindfold participants. Adult supervisors should be stationed at every area of the spook alley.

Monster Face Painting

Have children draw scary faces on each other with face paint. Have the children dress up and parade around to show others their costumes.

Ghost Stories

Take caution to make telling ghost stories a fun experience, not a terrifying one. Suspense is the key to a good ghost story. For children in an outdoor setting, it is more appropriate that a punch line or humorous ending is used, rather than a story that is going to continue to spook them as they walk back to their cabin.

Pumpkin Carving Contest

A pumpkin can be carved in many ways, and children should use their imagination to explore the possibilities. Stencils and specialized carving tools can be purchased, or you can use the old-fashioned method using a knife and a big spoon. Some children may prefer to paint their pumpkins with tempera paint or attach other garden vegetables like cucumbers, broccoli, or potatoes to the pumpkin with toothpicks. Give awards for creativity and design and always have adult supervision.

Ghost Carving Contest

Use half-gallon cubes of vanilla ice cream in cardboard containers to make ghostly shapes. Remove the ice cream from the carton and add candy, coconut, or nut toppings. This chilly and spooky treat can also be judged on best design or most clever use of ice cream.

Creating a Monster

A group of five children form a monster by holding onto each other to make one big monster with three legs and seven arms. They must then move 10 feet across the ground.

Mad Scientist Green Slime

The recipe for green slime requires the following items:
- Two eight-ounce bottles of white glue
- Two cups of warm water
- One packet of unsweetened green punch mix
- Two teaspoons of Borax®

Separate the items into two different containers:
- Green punch mix, one-third cup of warm water, and two bottles of glue
- One-and-two-thirds cups of water and two teaspoons of Borax.

Mix the two bowls together and knead the slime until it is soft and free of excess water.

Papier-Mache Monster Head

Children make papier-mache paste by mixing one part flour with two parts water until the mixture is the consistency of thick paste. More flour or water can be added to thin or thicken the paste. The children continue to mix the paste to get all of the lumps out.

They then add a few tablespoons of salt to help prevent mold. Then, the children spread the paste on strips of newspaper over an eight-inch air-filled balloon. After the papier-mache is dry, children can then paint the monster head with eyes, a nose, and a mouth. Yarn can be glued to the head to create monster hair.

Papier-Mache
Monster Head

Witch's Brew

Make a brew in a plastic cauldron with green gelatin and candy worms. Most plastic cauldrons have a small hole in the bottom, so prepare the gelatin in another container and serve it out of the cauldron. Place a small bowl in the cauldron to prevent gelatin from leaking out.

Untrick and Untreating

Most children are familiar with the Mad Hatter's version of celebrating an unbirthday, which entails celebrating all of the days of the year except the actual birthday of the individual. Using the same logic, an untrick and untreating activity involves dressing up in costumes and going to other people's houses, cabins, or tents with plastic pumpkins in hand and *giving* out candy instead of asking for it.

A Ghost in the Bottle

Freeze an empty glass soda or water bottle. After taking the bottle out of the freezer, have a child place a penny on top of the bottle opening and watch the magic as a drop of water hits the penny and makes it dance.

Program #9: Parachute Games

Cat and Mouse

Children are "mice" who hide under the parachute while one participant—the "cat"—tries to find the mice from on top of the parachute. When the cat finds the mice, he tries to catch them. The first mouse that is caught then comes out from underneath the parachute and is the cat for the next game.

Shark Attack

The group pretends they are "swimmers" as they sit with just their legs under the parachute, waiting for a shark attack. When the shark, who is hiding under the parachute, attacks, he grabs a child's legs and pulls him under. When a child is pulled under the parachute, he becomes a shark too. The swimmers are sitting down and can move around a little to avoid being caught. Two "lifeguards" can be appointed to "save" the swimmers by pulling them out of the parachute before they go completely under. The shark cannot keep pulling the swimmer when the lifeguard has a hold of the swimmer.

Make a Tent

Everyone lifts the parachute up as high as they can and then pulls it down behind them and sits on it from the inside. The parachute will make a tent for five to 10 minutes.

Pick a Color

As in the Make a Tent game, the children lift a multicolored parachute up and quickly pull it down to the ground. As the children are doing so, the leader calls out a color and everyone that is holding onto that color runs underneath the parachute before it reaches the ground and tries to find a vacant section of that same color. For example, if the leader yells yellow, all of the children holding onto a yellow section must run underneath the parachute, come out the other side, and find a new yellow section to hold onto.

Bounce the Ball

The children flap the parachute up and down while bouncing a ball or multiple balls on top. Have them see how high the balls can go.

Under the Big Top (Circus Tent)

Cover playground equipment with the parachute and let the children play inside like it's a circus.

Program #10: Crazy Frolics

Crazy Hair, Hats, and Backward Clothes

Have children find the weirdest hat to wear. Spike their hair, grease it up, or use a wire coat hanger to make ponytails go wacky. Have children wear their clothes backward or wear their pajamas all day. Children can have an amazing amount of fun with little or no expense.

Costume Party

Many children only dress in costumes for Halloween, so a simple costume party anytime of the year is a real treat. Parties can be themed, like a sock hop with 1950s-style poodle skirts and leather jackets, or the Roaring Twenties with zoot suites and flapper dresses.

Eat Lunch With Hands Tied Together

Serve a hamburger lunch with fries and a milkshake on a table where a group of eight people sit in a square. Tie each hand of each participant to someone else's hand at the table. The fun is when someone tries to eat and puts his hand to his month and the person on the other end of the rope tugs at the rope; food goes flying.

Finger Painting with Pudding

On a piece of white poster paper, have children finger paint using an assortment of colors and flavors of pudding.

Ugly Cake Decorating Contest

Have teams of children make and decorate ugly cakes, as long as they are still edible. Leave the rules a little vague regarding being edible. Frosting a cake with cottage cheese or guacamole dip makes it look ugly, but it is still edible! The inside of a yellow or white cake can be died red, black, or purple with food coloring. Awards for cakes can range from the ugliest cake, to honorable mention, to most likely to be found in a garbage can, etc.

Food Stunts with Healthy Foods

Have teams of children perform food stunts by eating spinach, broccoli, sardines, and brussels sprouts. Award points for quantity eaten, not speed.

Invent Crazy Words and Names

Have the children brainstorm fun names that sound like something else when the first and last names are put together. Examples include Tom Morrow, Jim Nasium, Poly Esther, Ilene Over, Ela Funt, Justin Case, and Harry Foote. Make a list of nonsense words or phrases. Ask silly questions. Why it is called a hot water heater when hot water doesn't need heating? Or, does to unthaw a rump roast mean to refreeze it? Or, where was the Declaration of Independence signed? At the bottom, of course! Look up words in the dictionary like balderdash, fiddle faddle, and poppycock.

Special Delivery Telegrams

Have children deliver singing telegrams for birthdays or deliver cupid grams, dressing in red and white clothes like a cupid and delivering love notes or Valentines to other children in the group.

Gelatin Slurping Contest

Give every participant a bowl of gelatin and a straw. Then, set the stopwatch and let children slurp the gelatin as fast as they can. The first participant to finish is the winner.

Program #11: Frontier Village

Lumberjack Larry's Base Camp

Using a small saw, have adults help children cut a circle section of a small branch. The adult leader can drill a small hole in the top and brand the wood with a branding iron. The child then strings plastic lace through the hole to make a wood necklace. Leaders give children beads or plastic bear or eagle claws at each station after the children complete each activity.

Coyote Joe's Mountain Man Rendezvous

Create a contest with tomahawks in a roped-off, or fenced, area for children over the age of 11. Use a wooden stump as a stand and set another stump on top, resting on its side. Adult leaders should give instructions on throwing. Tomahawks should be thrown using the forearm and not be thrown like a baseball. Metal-handle tomahawks are more durable than wooden-handle tomahawks. Tomahawks must be locked up when this activity is over.

Native American 3-D Archery Hunt

Set up a secured, roped-off archery area where children over the age of 12 can shoot at foam targets shaped as deer, bears, turkeys, or raccoons. Create an area where they can stand and listen to safety rules. Use certified and qualified archery leaders. Refer to Chapter 11, Program #89 for recommendations for setting up a 3-D archery range.

Native American Tepee

Have the children gather inside a tepee and have a leader tell a legend from a tribe within the local area. At the end of the story, give each child a turkey feather. Have leaders show different Native American dances outside the tepee.

Jedediah's Blacksmith Shop

Have children watch an adult leader as he bends horseshoes with fire, a hammer, and anvil. Leaders can also make prairie rings by shaping horseshoe nails into rings.

Prospector Pete's Panning for Gold Area

Cover the bottom of a large plastic container with sand and add water until it is half full. Add gravel, iron pyrite, and a bag of assorted gems and polished rocks. With prospecting pans and wooden-framed screens, teach children how to "pan" for gold.

Create a Dry Creek Frontier Town

Create a frontier town with full sheets of plywood. Secure each building to the ground with stakes and wire and decorate with paint. Use the following ideas for buildings and activities:

- Barber shop—Use face paint to add mustaches and beards.
- School—Teach arithmetic with small blackboard slates.
- Jail—Distribute small, inexpensive metal sheriff badges. Make "wanted" posters out of plywood that children can put their heads through and get their picture taken with a cowboy hat and bandanna.
- General Store—Give out jellybeans, licorice, candy sticks, horehound candy, and lemon drops.
- Fort—For children ages eight and older and with qualified and certified adults, set up a shooting gallery with airsoft guns to shoot at targets. Eye protection should be worn by all participants and spectators. The area needs to be roped off, with a red flag flying to indicate that a target range is open. Refer to Chapter 11, Program #87 for recommendations for setting up a target range.

Program #12: Circus

Create a Big Top Circus Tent

In an indoor setting, make a tent using crepe paper hung from the ceiling and taped to the walls. Use alternating colors for a special effect. Have children create clowns and circus animals with construction paper.

Clowns

Leaders and children can dress up as clowns. Use face paint, a multicolored rainbow wig, a foam nose, and big shoes to add to the look.

Clown Tag

The participant that is "it" chases the other children. When a player is tagged, he freezes in a silly clown position until someone else crawls under his legs to "free" him from the silly clown position.

Pie Throwing Activity

Fill an aluminum pie tin with a pie crust and whipping cream and have children line up to get a pie in the face. Helpful hints: Seek volunteers so this event doesn't get out of hand or make someone feel bad. Use a blindfold and have the participant hold his nose so whipping cream does not get into his eyes and nose. Gently press the pie into the participant's face and avoid throwing it. This technique provides a safer experience for the participant, and the pie can be used again for another child after simply refilling it with cream. Be aware of children with dairy-product allergies, and have them watch and not participate.

Tin Can Stilts

Make walking stilts from number 10 tin cans and rope. Punch holes in both sides of each can and run rope through them. Children can stand on the tin cans and lift up the rope as they walk on stilts.

Balloon Animals

Teach the basic techniques in making different balloon animals or hats. These techniques include the bubble and two-bubble twist, lock twist, loop twist, and pinch twist. You can make balloon poodles, hats, cats, rabbits, and giraffes with these basic twists.

Three Rings of Fun

Have children stand in a circle holding hands and passing a hoop (e.g., a Hula Hoop) around without breaking the hand grasps. Participants need to duck down and lift their legs to climb through the hoop as it is passed over them. When one hoop has successfully passed through the circle, introduce two more and have the hoops chase each other.

Candle and Squirt Gun Relay

With adult supervision, have children line up with squirt guns and try to extinguish the small flame on a candle three or four feet in front of them.

Teach Juggling

Teach basic techniques while juggling balls, silk scarves, rings, plates, and clubs.

Walking on Beams

Have children pretend they are tightrope walkers as they balance themselves on a two-by-four wooden beam lying on the ground. When participants are comfortable accomplishing that task, have them do it blindfolded. Make sure adults are close by to help children keep their balance. Secure the beam to the ground with tent pegs.

Circus Treats

Serve the following fun circus treats:
- Popcorn in paper bags
- A bag of peanuts
- Snow cones
- Lemonade
- Large lollipops

Unicycle Riding Workshop

Provide the opportunity for children to learn to ride a unicycle under close adult supervision and with protective head gear and protective padding.

Musical Chairs With Recorded Harpsichord Music

Have children form a circle of chairs with one fewer chair than participants. Start the harpsichord music and have participants walk along the empty chairs until the harpsichord music stops. Then, each participant races to sit in an empty chair. The participant who doesn't have a chair to sit in is out of the game until the next round. Leaders take one chair out at the end of each round.

3

Dreaming About Careers

Program #13: Rodeo Cowboy and Cowgirl

Roping Sawhorses With Lassos

Attach a fabric horse head from a stick horse or a plastic bull head purchased at a farm supply store to the end of a sawhorse. Teach children the proper way to use a lasso.

The Barrel Run

Make a triangle on a field or parking lot with three 55-gallon drums. Place the barrels approximately 50 feet away from each other. Each participant races by himself and against the clock. Leaders can announce on a blow horn as each participant races completely around each barrel, starting with the closest barrel on the right, then racing toward the barrel on the left, and then running for the third barrel at the tip of the triangle in a clover formation. During the entire race, the participant is holding a stick horse in his hand.

Homemade Stick Horses

To make a stick horse, cut a three-foot section of one-inch PVC pipe. Children can attach a large cotton-stuffed tube sock on one end of the pipe using duct tape. Buttons can be sewn on the sock for eyes, and fabric or yarn can be sewn on for the hair. They can make a bridle with a piece of rope tied around the nose and wrapped around the horse's neck. A loop is formed with the reins for the child to hold onto the horse. Adult

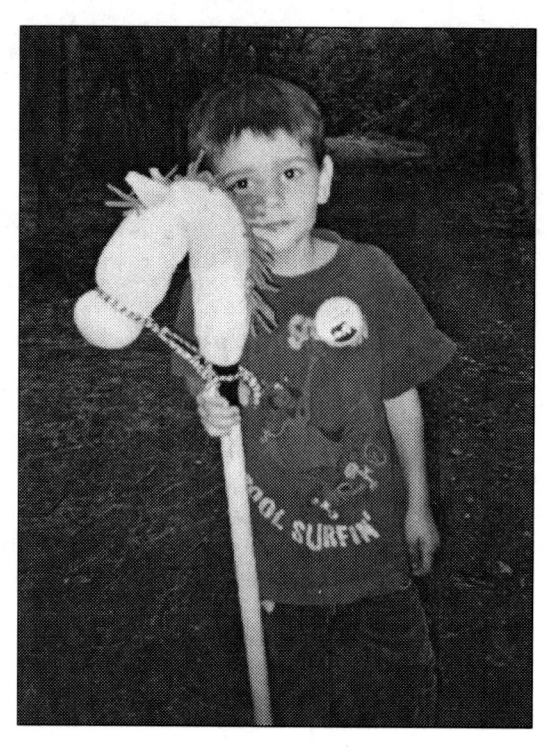

leaders should warn parents and children about the strangulation hazard when letting children play with the stick horse unattended.

Bicycle Rodeo

Perform a barrel race with bicycles, skateboards, or scooters. Make sure the children are wearing helmets, as well as knee and shoulder pads. For safety reasons, adults should determine how fast the participants should go based upon the ground conditions and other factors. Another bicycle activity is to put a raw egg on a cone and have children park their bikes as close to the cone as possible without tipping the egg over.

Wagon Race

Perform a barrel race with umbrella strollers with large teddy bears buckled in as passengers. The children push the strollers as fast as they can.

Potato Sack and Three-Legged Race

Have children climb into a potato sack and race each other. Or, have a three-legged race in which each team of two ties their center legs together with a bandanna and races the other teams.

Rodeo Clowns

Children can dress up in overalls, goofy foam cowboy hats, and big shoes and paint their faces like rodeo clowns.

Karaoke to Country Western Songs

Rent a karaoke machine and have children sing their favorite country western song. Adults should screen music beforehand and remove music with inappropriate lyrics.

Root Beer Drinking Contest

Children can have a root beer drinking contest, drinking from big glasses or two-liter bottles. Extra points are awarded for the longest or most original belch.

Bullwhip Balloon Pop Activity

This activity is designed for children over the age of 11. Using bullwhips, the children can pop large eight-inch balloons hanging from a stump that is placed on a platform approximately five feet off of the ground. Each participant should wear goggles and a thick jacket and only use the whip underhand. The sectioned-off area should be large, but allow enough room for only one person at a time to participate. All equipment should be locked up when the activity is over.

Horseshoe Competition

Adult leaders can set up a horseshoe pit where children toss horseshoes and try to get as close as possible to the post to earn points. The child or team with the most points at the end of the round wins the competition.

Program #14: Candy Factory Chocolatier

Hand Washing

Teach children the importance of hand washing when working with food by doing the following experiment, which teaches how germs are spread. Lightly dust one teaspoon of all-purpose flour on a piece of paper or a book. Have children pass around the item without telling them that anything is on it. One leader should put some flour on his hand and start shaking the children's hands. After spreading the flour around for a few minutes, turn off the overhead lights and shine a portable black light on all of the children's hands to see how much flour was spread around.

Chocolate Bars

Adult leaders purchase candy molds and melt either white or milk chocolate in a double boiler or microwave. Children can add sprinkles to the mold before they spoon in the chocolate. After filling the candy molds, freeze them for a few minutes. Children can also make chocolate suckers by putting chocolate in flat sucker molds and adding sticks.

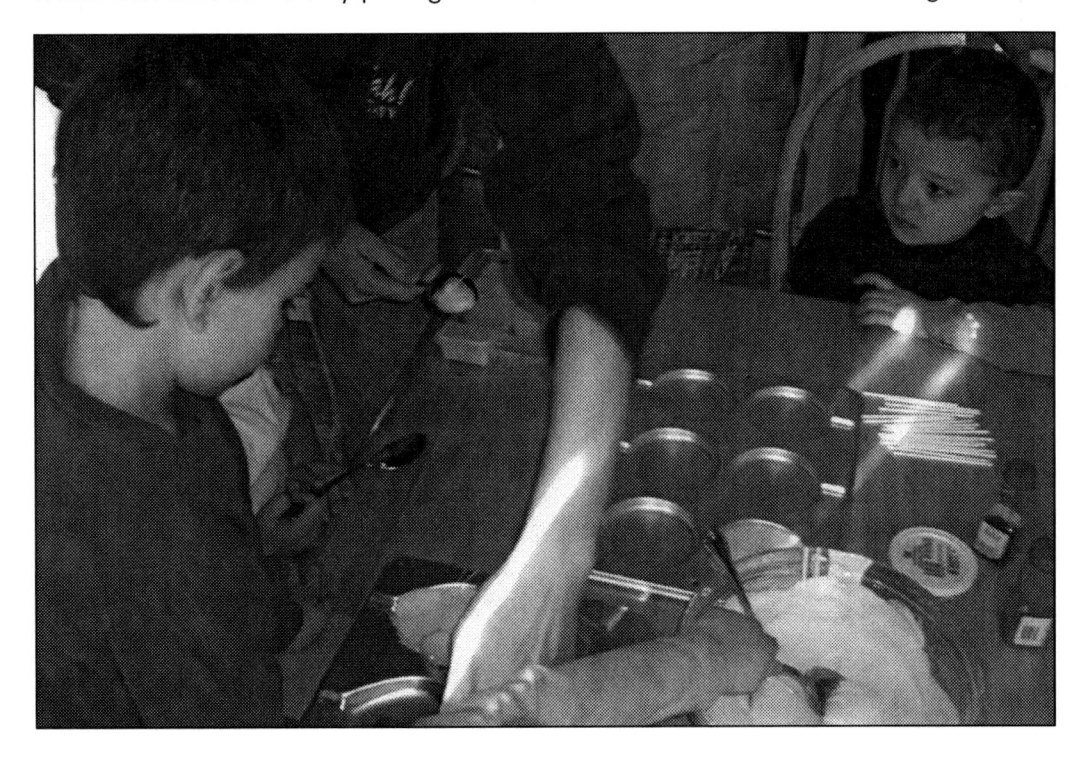

Guess How Many Jellybeans

Fill a jar to the top with jellybeans and put on the lid. Have the children guess how many jellybeans are in the jar to win a prize.

Bubble Blowing Contest

Give each child several pieces of nonstick bubble gum and have a contest to see who can blow the largest bubble.

Unwrapped Game

Children sit on the floor in a circle to play this game. Prior to the activity, an adult should wrap a candy bar in several layers of newspaper and tape it heavily with masking tape. At the beginning of the game, put a fork, a butter knife, and a pair of ski gloves in the center of the circle with the wrapped candy bar. Each participant rolls a pair of dice. If he rolls doubles, the participant puts the gloves on and starts to unwrap the candy bar using only the knife and fork before someone else rolls doubles. The winner is the participant who unwraps the rest of the newspaper off the candy bar, thereby winning the candy bar.

Sticky Situation

Explain to the group that an explosion of marshmallow fudge took place at the candy factory. Each group of six people is "stuck" together with bandannas. Tie their arms and legs together and have the group try to safely move across the room.

Jawbreaker Relay

Fill four gallon-size buckets with balls, which the children can pretend are gigantic jawbreakers, using a different type of ball in each bucket (tennis balls, golf balls, small plastic footballs, and ping pong balls). At the beginning of the game, dump all four buckets of balls in one big pile and mix them around. The group will be timed on how fast they can sort out the balls by type and put them back in the original buckets.

Who Stole the Candy From the Candy Jar?

In this game, a group of participants sits on the ground in a circle with their legs folded and claps in rhythm to the following phrases, which are spoken by two members of the group:

"Who stole the candy from the candy jar?" (He would then say someone else's name.)

"_____ stole the candy from the candy jar."

"Who, me?"

"Yes, you."

"Couldn't be!"

"Then who?"

The second person would then say another person's name and serve as the first person in the next round.

Peppermint Candy and the Brown Sugar Tower

Form a small tower of brown sugar by tightly packing a cup of brown sugar and flipping it over onto a table. Place a peppermint candy on top. Each participant is given a plastic knife and takes turns trimming off a slice of the brown sugar tower without knocking the peppermint off. The person who knocks the peppermint off the tower is awarded the pile of brown sugar, and everyone else in the group receives a peppermint candy.

LifeSavers® Relay

Have the group separate into teams of equal size, with each team standing in a straight line. Participants hold a sucker stick in their hand to pass a LifeSavers candy to the person behind them. The team that has successfully passed the candy to each team member wins the relay. Sucker sticks can be purchased in bulk at craft stores.

Candy Bar Tag

The participant that is "it" chases other children and tries to tag them before they can say a name of a candy bar. After a candy bar is mentioned, it cannot be used again. Once a participant is tagged, he is out of the game until a new round.

Program #15: Grand Prix Racecar Driver

The Human Racecar Relay

Human racecars are made up of four people, each representing a wheel of the car and holding a hoop (e.g., a Hula Hoop). Each participant rolls his hoop on the ground while the team runs together toward the finish line. Human racecars compete against the clock to determine which racecar is the winner.

Cars and Trucks

Have four participants stand on a telephone pole that is lying secure on the ground so that it doesn't move. They should face the other team of four participants, who are also standing on the telephone pole. Label one team "cars" and the other team "trucks" and have them trade places without stepping off the pole and into the pretend "hot tar." If someone does step off, both teams need to start over.

Pit Stop Eating Relay

Dangle several glazed donuts from strings suspended from a broom stick held up by two leaders. Each participant chooses one donut, which represents a tire to be changed during a grand prix pit stop. Each child tries to eat the donut faster than the other participants.

Remote Control Car Race

Set up a racetrack with cones and race six remote control cars around the course. Each car needs to be on a different frequency. Another method is to race one car against the clock. Participants can use the same car, as long as a new battery is used with each new participant. The racer with the fastest time wins the race.

Scooter Race

Hold scooter races in which participants race against the clock and perform a series of maneuvers in an obstacle course. Have participants wear the proper headgear and pads.

Soapbox Derby—A New Twist on an Old Favorite

Have each participant strap an unopened three-pound box of laundry soap to a skateboard using bungee cords and roll the box down a hill or through a parking lot. The soapbox that crosses the finish line first wins.

Racecar

Shape a car out of a block of Styrofoam™ or a piece of wood and attach plastic wheels with small nail axles. Color the cars with paint and add racing stripes and stickers.

Design Smoking Hot Racecar

Under close adult supervision, children ages 10 and older can create their dream cars with a flat piece of wood and a wood-burning kit. For best results, draw the image in pencil first and follow the pencil lines with the wood burner to create the image.

Ice Blocking Race

Purchase large blocks of ice and use them as sleds to slide down a small grassy hill. Place a towel over the ice to prevent a freezing effect as participants sit on the ice.

Banana Split

Children can decorate a banana as a racecar by gluing (using nontoxic white glue) a paper racing number, a paper windshield, and a toy driver onto the banana. Then, they can attach four plastic wheels with small nail axles. The children can have a banana split racing contest after they make their racecars.

Model Racecar Kit

With inexpensive "snap on" car model kits that do not require glue or painting, design an activity in which children assemble racecars on a large table that resembles a car-manufacturing plant. Adults should assist children in putting together their model racecars.

Program #16: Chef

Chili Cook-Off

Divide the group into cooking teams. Provide basic ingredients to make chili, but allow the groups to add some of their own adult-approved "secret" ingredients, such as root beer, to make the contest interesting. Adult leaders can be the judges to determine which team made the best chili. Blue ribbons or trophies should be awarded by the judges.

Watermelon Eating Contest

Cut watermelon into half-moon-shaped pieces and have children race against each other to see who can finish the fastest.

Chocolate Pudding Drop

Divide children into pairs and have one participant lay on the ground with his mouth open. The other participant stands on a chair and attempts to feed chocolate pudding to his partner by dropping spoonfuls into his mouth. The team that finishes the bowl of pudding with the least amount of mess is the winner.

Cake Decorating Contest

Teach children to design cakes. Give each child a cake to decorate and frosting to make cake designs such as flowers and special borders. Have the children display their cakes for judging. Afterward, hold a silent auction of the cakes as a fundraiser.

Cooking Workshop

Have chefs from local restaurants teach workshops on preparing restaurant-quality food. Children can learn to follow a recipe to make their favorite foods. Have a food-service employee teach the children how to set a table and give serving tips such as serving the food from the left and picking up the food from the right. Teach children good eating habits by having them create a healthy menu for a pretend restaurant.

Setting the Table

Have the children sit in a circle on the ground with place settings in front of them. The person who has been chosen to start the game tells the participant on his left, "This is a spoon," as he hands the spoon to the second person. The second person questions, "A what?" "A spoon," restates the first person. Then, the second person repeats the same dialogue to the person on his left and the conversation continues throughout the circle. Meanwhile, the first person brings out a knife and tells the person on his left, "This is a knife." The process continues with a fork, glass, and plate. The fun of this game is the confusion that occurs when trying to keep the place settings straight.

Eat Crackers and Whistle

Have children determine who can eat three saltine crackers the fastest and whistle a short song afterward.

Vegetable Soup Relay

Have 13 participants lie on the ground and use their bodies to spell out the words "vegetable soup" as fast as they can.

Table Bussing

In teams of two, one child holds a bucket as the other child tosses plastic knives, forks, and spoons from the table into the bucket. The team that gets the most items in the bucket the fastest wins the game.

Program #17: Secret Spy

Mission #1—Find the Spy

Give one leader a plastic spoon to put in his pocket, which indicates that he is the spy. All the leaders hide and the children seek after them. When participants find an adult, they ask to see the spoon. If the adult leader doesn't have the spoon, the participants continue searching for the spy with the spoon.

Mission #2—Secret Message

This activity is designed for children age 12 and older. Put a piece of paper with a secret message in one balloon and then fill it with air and tie it on a string connected to two poles or trees. Add several other air-filled balloons to the target range and have children pop the balloons with slingshots to find the message. For safety reasons, have adult supervision and have children wear eye protection. Make sure the children do not run into the target range to find the secret message until after everyone is finished shooting and the adult leader gives a vocal command to retrieve the balloons. Refer to Chapter 11, Program #90 for recommendations on setting up a slingshot range. All equipment must be locked up when the activity is over.

Mission #3—Marshmallow Capture the Flag

Make a marshmallow shooter with a one-and-a-half-foot-long, half-inch-diameter PVC pipe for each participant. Divide the group into two teams and have them play capture the flag with mini-marshmallows. The defending team blows mini-marshmallows with their shooters at their opponents instead of tagging them. Instruct participants not to run with the pipe in their mouths or store marshmallows in their mouths. Wash and sanitize the shooters before each game. After this activity, participants need to clean all marshmallows off of the ground.

Mission #4—"Nuclear Waste" Removal

Fill an empty clear two-liter soda bottle with water and green food coloring to make "nuclear waste." Place the bottle on a circular wooden platform that is two feet in diameter and attached to several long pieces of rope. The team members move the platform from one location to another by each lifting a section of the rope. The team takes the nuclear waste bottle across the room to the new location. Anytime the bottle falls off the platform, the team needs to start over.

Mission # 5—Spider in the Bag

Ask a volunteer to put his hand in a paper bag with a kiwi fruit at the bottom. Tell the volunteer that a tarantula is sitting at the bottom of the bag. See who is willing to pick the spider out of the bag.

Mission #6—Secret Code

Have the group stand in single file facing straight ahead. Give the first participant a secret code and have him repeat it to the next person in line and continue the procedure until the secret code gets to the last person in line. He then repeats the code out loud. The group compares it to the original secret code.

Mission #7—I Spy

One participant selects something nearby that everyone else can see and then says, "I spy with my little eye something that is _____." The rest of the group searches until they have identified the item. The first participant to identify the item selects something else to "spy."

Mission #8—Invisible Ink

Using either lemon juice or milk as ink and a pipe cleaner as a pen, write messages that only can be read when the paper is near heat, such as a 100-watt light bulb. To prevent injuries, children should not put the paper or their hands too close to the light bulb.

Program #18: Soldier

Leaders can purchase inexpensive dog tags from a party supply store and have each child's name stamped on the tag. Children can wear them around their necks during each soldier day activity.

Drill Sergeant's Callisthenic Game

Have the group form a line facing the drill sergeant. This activity is played just like "Simon Says." The drill sergeant gives commands for calisthenics that start with "drill sergeant says." If the command does not start off with "drill sergeant says," the participants should not perform the task or they will be out of the game. For example, if the leader says, "Drill sergeant says do jumping jacks," then each participant should do jumping jacks. If the leader says, "Run in place," anyone who starts running in place is out of the game.

Operation Blindfolded Twine Hike

Rope off a short hike through the trees with waist-high twine that can be used as a handrail. Each participant is blindfolded and can only use the twine to find his way back to base camp. For a special effect, create some paths that lead off from the main path and become a dead end, thereby causing a short diversion.

Operation Dodgeball

Divide the group into two teams and have them face each other. Put several playground balls in the center of the playing court. Teams line up on a starting line on their side of the court. As the leader yells, "Go!" both teams race toward the center line to retrieve the balls without stepping over the line. Participants throw playground balls at each other. When someone gets hit, he joins the opposing team. Participants should not aim for the heads of their opponents. When one team "wins" over all of their opponents, the game is over.

Operation Reconnaissance Mission

Send a participant out of the room while you hide a small item. When the participant comes back into the room, the rest of the group can only tell the participant if he is "hot" or "cold" in finding the hidden object. As the participant gets nearer to the object, he becomes "hotter." If he is far away from the object, he is "cold as ice."

KP Duty—Leaky Garbage Container

Set two plastic garbage containers on a grassy field. One garbage container should have several holes in it. The other garbage container is filled with water. Participants begin dipping small buckets into the garbage container that is full of water and start filling the garbage container that has holes in it. Participants should think of ways to plug the holes of the leaky garbage container. One method is to have a participant sit inside the leaky container to plug some of the holes while other team members plug the holes from the outside.

Operation Frisbee Knock

Participants throw a Frisbee at cones set in a pyramid to try to knock them over. Only one participant can throw a Frisbee at a time and the next participant in line cannot throw until the previous Frisbee is retrieved. The game is finished when the participants have knocked all the cones down.

Operation Minefield

Section off a 12-foot square area with a rope placed on the ground. Put 50 tennis balls within the square. Divide the teams in half, with partners standing on opposite sides of the rope square. One participant will be blindfolded and act like a tank driving blindly through the minefield. The other participant will act as the driver and navigate the tank through the minefield with vocal commands.

Operation Human Tank

Connect the ends of a 30-inch-wide by 39-feet-long piece of durable vinyl mat to form a large band. Participants get inside the band and walk, with the lead participant pulling the mat down to keep it moving forward. The band functions like the giant wheel of a tank. Set up a 100-foot long course with cones for the human tank to maneuver though.

Operation Spider's Web

Tie several strains of twine between two trees in a four-foot section to look like a giant spider's web. Participants climb through the holes in the web with the help of their teammates. Participants cannot touch the twine as they cross through the web or the whole team has to start over. Each team member has to go through a different hole in the spider's web for the team to complete the task.

Operation Tall Tower

Divide the group into two teams and give each team a can of Tinkertoys®. The team that builds that tallest free-standing tower in five minutes win.

Operation Obstacle Course

Set up an obstacle course in which individual participants race against the clock through the following obstacles:

- Hurdles—Set two cinder blocks on their ends and place a two-by-four board on top. Set up a row of five hurdles that participants have to jump over.
- Letter Plates—Write each letter of the alphabet on a small plastic plate. Mix up the plates and have the participants organize the plates in alphabetical order.
- A Frame—Build a four-foot "A" frame structure by connecting two half-sheets of plywood together with a wooden support structure underneath. Cut small handholds in the plywood so that participants can climb up one side and climb down the other side.
- Tire Chain—Place six tires together in two rows. Participants must straddle the tires as they run through them.
- Ping Pong Drop—After folding a bed sheet into a funnel with a wide top and a narrow bottom, participants use the funnel to try to put 10 ping pong balls into an empty tennis ball container. If all of the balls do not go into the container, the participant has to start over.
- Rope Jump—Place two ropes on the floor parallel to each other with a three-foot gap in between. Participants jump over the gap and land over the top of the second rope.
- Izzy Dizzy—Each participant holds a baseball bat perpendicular to the ground and places his forehead on the top by bending toward the bat. He then runs in a circle around the bat 10 times with his head still on the bat and runs toward the finish line of the obstacle course.

Program #19: Astronaut

Moon Ball

Have the group try to keep a beach ball from touching the ground. For more of a challenge, have participants touch the ball in order so that no one can touch the ball twice until everyone in the group has touched it once. Add some balloons as "stars" that the group has to keep up at the same time.

Asteroid Ball

Have the group walk across the room while keeping the beach ball in the air like an asteroid moving through the galaxy. Set up a course with cones that the team has to travel through.

Spaceship Landing

Cover some playground equipment with a couple of blankets and pretend it is a spaceship. Have participants land the spaceship on a new planet. After landing the spaceship, astronauts walk around the planet collecting rock and plant specimens to take back to Earth. An adult leader dressed as an alien should greet the astronauts and present them with a special flying saucer treat (refer to the next activity).

Flying Saucer Treat

Serve green gelatin in a small foil pie tin. Have a small bubble container with an alien toy inside (usually found in a gumball machine). Decorate the outside of the foil pie tin with candy and frosting to make it look like the lights of a spaceship.

Solar System in Sidewalk Chalk

After drawing the sun, moon, some stars, satellites, asteroids, space shuttle, the international space station, and all of the planets, spend time visiting each drawing. Teach the children about each drawing and why it is an important part of our solar system.

Fixing a Satellite in Space

Put the team of children ages 12 and older in an imaginary space station and tell them that they need to fix a broken satellite. To access the satellite, the astronauts need to cross a special bridge. The bridge is made of several cinder blocks, and each block needs to be touched by an astronaut or it will disappear into space. For the team to leave the space station, they must hand a block to the first person, who then steps on the block. The team then adds more blocks to make a bridge. If anyone loses contact with a block, the adult leader removes that block. After the team completes the mission, they must return the blocks to the space station.

Paper Rocket Launching

Children wrap colored copy paper around a 15-inch-long piece of half-inch PVC pipe. They use a hot glue gun to connect both sides of the paper; leaders should supervise children as they use a hot glue gun for their rockets. Once the two sides of the paper have been connected, the PVC pipe is removed. Participants can put designs on their paper. A piece of foam "noodle" can be cut and shaped into a nosecone and placed at the tip of the rocket. Once the rocket is made, an adapted air launcher will shoot the rocket 50 or more feet in the air (refer to the next activity).

Paper Rocket Air Launcher

To make a launcher, adults cut all of the lengths of PVC and sand the ends to get rid of burs. Drill a half-inch hole in one of the two-inch caps and pop the tubeless tire valve into the hole. Use primer and cement to join each slip joint. (To allow for disassembly, do not cement threaded pieces.) The three-quarter-inch "T" coupling should be aimed upward to hold the launch rod assembly. Make sure that when you connect the in-line sprinkler valve you have the arrows pointing up. Cut the remaining half-inch pipe into 15-inch lengths to build the paper rockets. Children will place their paper rocket on the two-foot long pipe. Then they attach a bike pump to the launcher's tire valve and pump approximately 10 times to build enough pressure for the rocket. They then release the air pressure by opening the switch of the in-line sprinkler valve, blasting the rocket high into space.

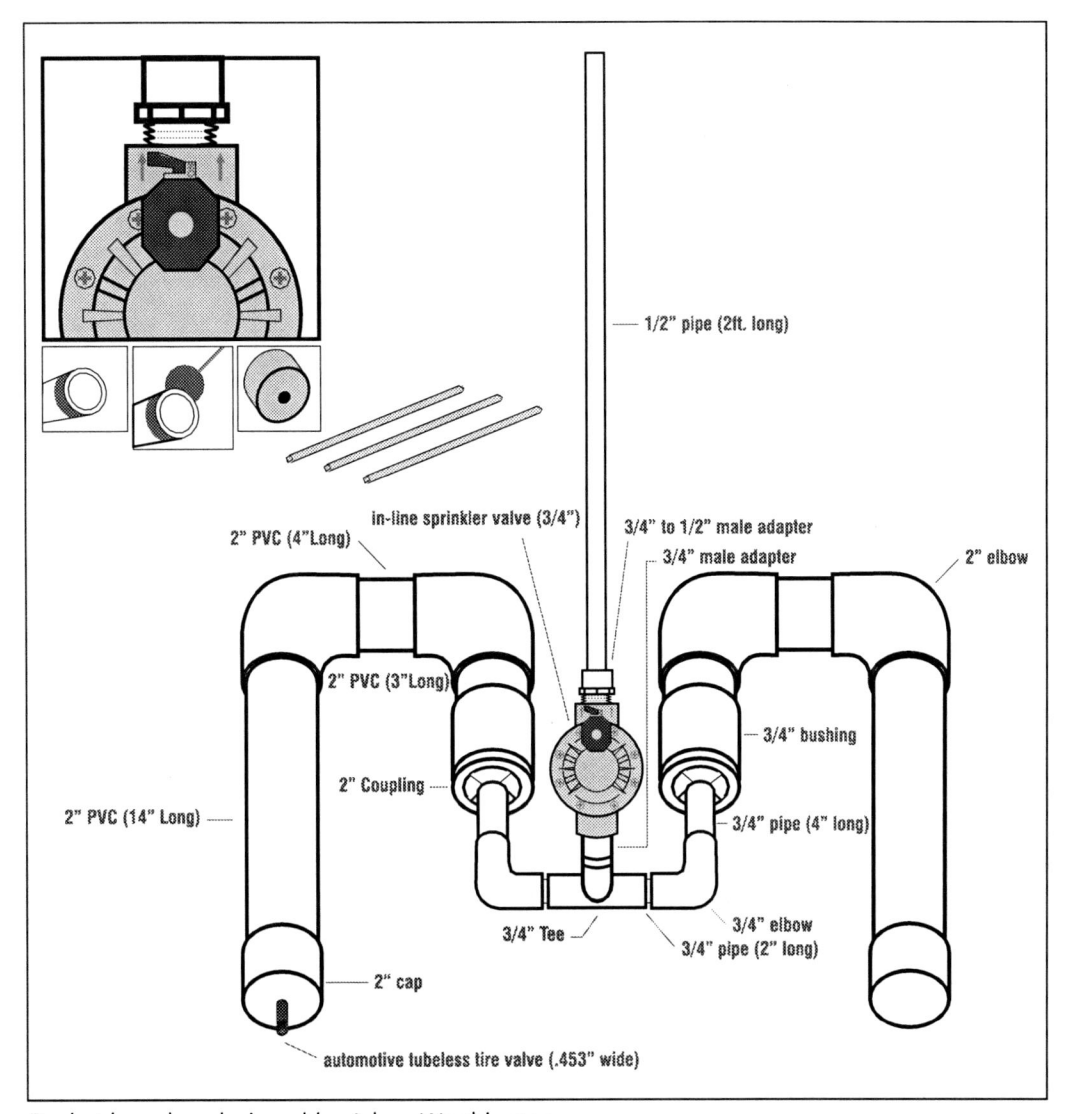

- 1/2" pipe (2ft. long)
- in-line sprinkler valve (3/4")
- 3/4" to 1/2" male adapter
- 3/4" male adapter
- 2" PVC (4"Long)
- 2" elbow
- 2" PVC (3"Long)
- 3/4" bushing
- 2" Coupling
- 2" PVC (14" Long)
- 3/4" pipe (4" long)
- 3/4" Tee
- 3/4" elbow
- 3/4" pipe (2" long)
- 2" cap
- automotive tubeless tire valve (.453" wide)

Rocket launcher designed by Adam Worthington

Program #20: Farmer

Pin the Tail on the Donkey

Blindfold a participant and spin him around a few times. The dizzy participant then makes his way to a large picture of a donkey and tries to pin a paper tail to the donkey. The participant who pins the tail closest to the donkey's tail wins.

Farm Animal Spin the Bottle

Have participants sit on the ground in a circle. A participant spins a glass bottle in the center of the circle. When the bottle stops, the person it is pointing to needs to make a farm animal sound as determined by the spinner of the bottle.

Duck, Duck, Goose

Participants sit in a circle on the ground. One participant starts walking behind the group, patting the heads of other participants and saying either "duck" or "goose." If this participant says "Duck," he continues patting the heads of the team, but if he says "Goose," the person whose head was patted jumps up and gives chase. If the participant being chased runs around the circle and sits down in the chaser's empty seat, he is safe. But if he gets tagged before he sits down, he is eliminated from this round of the game.

Barn Building

Set up two logs lying end to end. Place the same number of nails and a hammer on each log. Two participants compete to see who can hammer all of the nails into the log first.

Pig in the Pit

Create a large "pit" by placing a rope on the ground to mark off a 10-foot circle. Place a toy pig in the center of the pit and have the team figure out how to retrieve the pig without stepping into the pit or moving their rope. The team cannot use any resources except themselves and what they are wearing.

Pig Tail Contest

Have a pig tail contest for participants with long enough hair. Have awards for the longest pig tail, the best braid, and the craziest design.

Petting Zoo

Arrange with a local farmer to bring rabbits, goats, or lambs for the children to pet and feed. Also, plan a field trip to a farm or petting zoo.

Milking Contest

Place a thick green rubber glove on a canning jar full of milk. Use several rubber bands to secure the glove to the jar. Puncture a small hole in the glove and have participants squeeze the glove and squirt milk into a small bucket. Participants can compete against each other to determine who can fill the bucket first.

Purple Cow

Serve several scoops of vanilla ice cream in a large glass and fill the glass up with Concord grape juice.

Bulldog

One participant stands in the middle of the room or field and is "it." All the other people are lined up at one end of the room. The participant that is "it" yells out "bulldog," at which point all of the other people try to run to the other end without being caught. If someone is caught, he joins the person in the middle and then they work together to try to capture all of the other participants. The process goes on until only one person is left who hasn't been caught.

Run Sheep Run

Two teams play against each other and have the same home base. While one team hides, the other team searches for them. One member of the hiding team (the sheep) goes along with the searching team (the sheepdogs) and gives the signal of "run sheep run" when he feels that the sheepdogs are not looking. Upon hearing "run sheep run," the sheep run back to home base before the other team. The sheepdogs can also call "run sheep run" when they find anyone who is hiding and then they try to outrun the sheep back to home base. If the sheep make it back before the sheepdogs, they can stay sheep for the next round. If the sheepdogs make it back first, they become the sheep for the next round.

Early Bird Gets the Worm

One participant is a chicken and six other children make up the body of an earthworm by forming a line, with each participant holding onto the waist of the person in front of him. The participant at the front of the line is the head of the worm and tries to sway back and forth and goes in circles to protect the tail of the worm from getting tagged by the chicken. If the last person gets tagged by the chicken, he becomes the head of the worm and the tail of the worm becomes the chicken.

Grunt Piggy Grunt

Blindfold the children and have them sit on chairs in a circle. Designate one person as the "piggy." The piggy sits on someone's lap and grunts like a pig. The person he is sitting on has to guess who the piggy is.

Milk Bubbles

Give children small containers of milk and straws and let them blow milk bubbles with the straws all over the table. Let the children clean up their own mess with paper towels.

Program #21: Being a Grown Up

Dress Up

Fill a box with adult clothes that children can use to dress up. Provide an assortment of fun items including bow ties, necklaces, hats, boots, and high-heel shoes. Provide each child with a purse or wallet and put some play money inside. Adult clothes can be purchased at a thrift store.

Role Play

Select different adult roles such as a mother, father, or grandparent, and have children act them out. Leaders should make a list of what is included in a typical day for an employee, homemaker, or college student. Leaders can also talk about the need to balance adult responsibilities such as work, raising a family, yard- and housework, volunteering in the community, and exercise. Leaders should also emphasize the importance of preparing for adulthood by encouraging the children to do the following activities while they are still young:

- Play—Gaining social skills by playing with others
- Service—Helping others by sharing and doing nice things for other people
- Work—Learning responsibility by completing assigned tasks
- Hobbies—Finding interests that may develop into educational or career opportunities

The Game of Life® and Monopoly® Board Games

These games teach—in a fun way—about the choices and accountability that adults face each day in family life and in their careers. Children learn math and organizational skills as they play these games.

Make Money

Provide the opportunity for children to make money and then teach them about budgets and savings. Running a lemonade stand, making a craft and selling it, doing yard work, and cleaning are simple tasks that children can do to learn the importance of hard work and spending money wisely.

Set Up a Store

Provide some "program dollars" that children earn for accomplishing certain tasks. Being on time to scheduled activities and arriving at activities with the expected items (such as hats, sunscreen, daypacks, water bottles, or parent permission slips) are just two ways to earn dollars. Other ways to earn "program dollars" are sharing, including others in activities, and helping set up and clean up activities. Program dollars are pieces of paper that can be redeemed at the program store, where leaders have several small, inexpensive items for sale.

Personal Mission Statements and Goals

Provide the opportunity for children to set goals of what they want to accomplish in life and to create personal mission statements or rules to live by.

Program #22: News Reporter

Computer Keyboard

Cut one-foot square planks of plywood and paint one letter of the alphabet on each piece. Place these planks on the ground, organized as if they comprised a huge computer keyboard. Have one participant at a time run and jump on one of the computer keys, which are the wooden planks. Participants need to touch different keys. Before the next participant touches a computer key, the previous participant needs to be completely off the keyboard. The group should work against the clock to see how fast they can touch all of the keys on the keyboard without touching the same key twice. When the group has practiced using the computer keyboard with their feet, advance the game and give them a sentence to type using this same method. Write the sentence on a large poster board and time the group to see how fast they can type.

Nine Magazines

Place nine news magazines on a table in rows of three. Have a participant leave the room while the rest of the group chooses one magazine that will be the featured cover story. When the participant comes back into the room, the leader will point to each magazine and ask him which magazine has the featured cover story. The participant who left the room tries to guess which magazine it is. The trick to this game is the placement of the hand of the leader as he points to the magazine. If the leader points to the upper right side of a magazine, that magazine has the featured cover story. Otherwise, the leader will point to the lower left side of the magazines.

Breaking News—Eggs that Drop

Divide the group into smaller teams. Each team is given 20 straws, 36 inches of masking tape, a raw egg, and a 20-minute time limit. Have team members design a protective cover for the egg so it will be insulated when dropped from a height of 12 feet. The team with an uncracked egg wins the contest. Only adult leaders should drop the eggs.

Digging for the Truth

Each participant receives a potato and has five minutes to memorize every detail of the potato so that he can recognize it later. After five minutes, the leader collects all of the potatoes and puts them in a burlap sack, shaking them around. When the leader is finished shaking the potatoes, the potatoes are poured out onto the floor and each participant needs to find his own potato.

The Power of a Newspaper

Give each participant a standard sheet of copy paper and have him design a tower that will support a heavy book three inches off the table. After struggling with this task for a few minutes, each participant is given a rubber band and told to start over. By rolling the paper in a roll and wrapping a rubber band around it like a newspaper, the heavy book, which represents the learning opportunities provided by reading, can be supported.

Top Story—The Building of a Bridge

Divide the group into smaller teams and give each team a different brown paper bag full of resources. In one bag are 30 mini-marshmallows; in another bag are 18 toothpicks; in the last bag are 15 square crackers. Each team has 10 minutes to build a bridge over a piece of blue copy paper that represents a river. Groups can share resources only after they ask to. The marshmallows represent cement, the toothpicks represent steel beams, and the square crackers represent pavement. The teams can only build a bridge if they work together and don't compete with each other.

Calligraphy Workshop

Teach children to write their names in calligraphy and explain that communication prior to the invention of the computer and typewriter was done by hand. Show replicas of important hand-written historical documents like the United States Constitution, the Bill of Rights, and the Gettysburg Address.

Television News Report

Have the children make a home video news report with anchors behind the desk and field reporters on location. Include a weather, traffic, and sports report. Stories can be pretend or they can be actual stories from camp, school, and the neighborhood.

Program #23: Train Engineer

Model Trains

Set up a model train and let children play and explore the world of model trains. Trains can either be electric or wooden. Add little houses, cars, trees, and people to the train set. Purchase inexpensive engineer hats and wooden train whistles for each child.

Train Yard

Visit a train yard or a historic train depot. Visit with engineers and other employees to see what a typical day is like for those who work with trains professionally.

Cardboard Train Costume

Children can design train engines and cars using several large cardboard boxes and tempera paint. Have them place a box upside down and use the bottom of the box as the roof of the train. They can then cut windows in each of the cars and a circle out of the roof for a child's head. Use aluminum pie plates for the wheels. Each child wears a different part of the train: engine, coal car, box car, and caboose, and the group chugs around the room pretending to be a train.

Human Train

Children do not need costumes to pretend they are a train. They can do it by acting out all of the responsibilities of a train. The child who is the engine makes whistle noises. One child who is a boxcar carries lions and tigers and makes roaring sounds. Another child is the boxcar that carries alarm clocks and makes ticking sounds. The child who is the conductor repeats, "All aboard," and "Tickets, please."

I Am Going on a Train Trip

A leader starts this game by announcing, "I am going on a train and I am taking with me je*ll*ybeans," or any other item that has two of the same letters together. Examples include: green beans, a*pp*les, trees, ba*ll*s, and sleeping bags. After the leader states that he is going on a train trip, each child takes a turn by repeating the phrase, "I am going on a train trip and I am taking with me. . ." The child tries to guess what word will allow them on board the train. If the item does not have two of the same letters together, the leader states, "Sorry, you cannot come, try again next turn." This game continues until everyone figures out how to get on the train.

Graham Cracker Train

Allow the children to design a candy train with graham crackers and extra thick frosting. They can use an ice cream sugar cone for the smokestack and add candy cargo to each boxcar. They can also make train wheels with peppermint candy and a train track with licorice and pretzels.

Program #24: Movie Star

World Premiere

Dress the children in sunglasses, hats, and feather boas and have them walk down a red carpet with people taking their pictures and asking for autographs. Show a children's movie and make popcorn and serve boxed candy. Children can also make a cardboard car prior to the activity and turn the room into a drive-in theater.

Grauman's Chinese Theatre Footprint Ceremony

Pretend to be at Grauman's Chinese Theatre. Have the children take off their shoes and put their feet and hands in an aluminum pie plate full of wet plaster of Paris. Then, have them sign their names next to the handprints and footprints. Be sure to give each child a wet towel to wipe off their hands and feet. When the plaster of Paris is dry, remove it from the aluminum pie plate.

Celebrity Look-Alike Contest

Each child should pick a movie star and dress up like that star. Have a contest and awards for the best celebrity look-alikes. Call the special panel of judges that selects the contest winners the "Academy," so when children receive their awards they can "thank the Academy."

Sound Effects

The following household objects can be used to make special sound effects:
- Horse galloping—Hitting two halves of an empty coconut against the ground
- Rain drops—Dropping dried peas in an aluminum can
- Thunder—Shaking a sheet of thin metal back and forth
- Gun shot—Slapping two leather belts against each other
- Bear growl—Using a number-10 tin can with a cotton rope tied to a hole in the top of the can, apply molasses to the rope and rub it in to form a strong grip. Pull the rope and the vibrations from the rope will project a growling sound from the can.
- Clock ticking—Alternate tapping pencils on a table
- Fire—Crinkling cellophane or an empty plastic water bottle
- Cork popping—Clicking the tongue against the roof the mouth
- Telephone or doorbell—Ringing a bicycle bell
- Walking through grass—Rubbing the palms of the hands together

Name That Movie

Divide the group into two teams. The leader plays the first few seconds of a movie soundtrack and the teams compete to identify the movie first.

Guess Who I Am

Write a famous movie star's name on a strip of paper and tape it to the participant's back. By asking only "yes" and "no" questions, the participant must figure out whose name is on the strip of paper.

There's No Business Like Show Business

Teach children the song "There's No Business Like Show Business" from the play *Annie Get Your Gun*.

Program #25: Florist

Flower-Arranging Workshop

Provide a flower-arranging workshop during which children can learn how to arrange flowers and keep them looking fresh.

Silk Flower Arrangement

Give children several silk flowers to arrange in either a basket with a block of foam or a glass bowl with several glass stones to support the flowers.

Dried Flower Arrangement

Provide the opportunity for children to make a wreath using dried wildflowers.

Flower Delivery

With help from adult leaders, children can deliver flowers to a hospital or nursing home to feel the impact flowers can have on people in difficult situations. Children can also anonymously place flowers on headstones in a cemetery so that they can acquire a quiet respect for of those who have died.

Grow Flowers From Seeds

Give each child a packet of flower seeds such as sunflowers, petunias, or marigolds and have them plant them in a flowerpot. Set up a schedule so that children know when to

water the seeds. Teach them the difference between annuals and perennials, and how to care for both. Children will also need to learn about plant food and potting soils.

House Plants Stewardship

Give each child a small house plant in a terracotta pot and teach them plant-care tips. Have them paint and design their terracotta pot.

Pressed-Flowers Bookmark

Have the children make a bookmark with pressed flowers. Use either a large book or a flower press to preserve fresh flowers. Place them on strips of clear contact paper and fold the sticky side of the contact paper over. With a single-hole paper punch, add a hole to the top of the bookmark and tie a two-inch ribbon through the hole.

Wildflower Nature Walk

Children can take a wildflower guidebook and a sketch pad into the forest to identify and draw flowers that they see. Talk about preserving flowers in the wild so others can enjoy them.

State Flowers of the United States

Have children draw and color all of the state flowers in the United States, such as New Hampshire's purple lilac, Kentucky's goldenrod, and Arizona's saguaro cactus blossom. Have the children research each flower to learn why it is significant to each of the states.

4

Appreciating Nature

Program #26: Hikes

Cat Eye Hike

Attach several small bicycle reflectors or reflector tape to trees, fence posts, rocks, and bushes during the day. Participants that go on a night hike will be guided by the reflectors as they shine their flashlights around. Place the reflectors in pairs so that they look like animal eyes. Reflectors should be in close proximity to each other so participants can find the next location within a few steps of the previous one.

Magnifying Glass Hike

Section off a 10-foot square and have children look through magnifying glasses to see as many small items and insects as possible. Make a list of each child's findings.

Leaky Backpack

Section off a 15-feet-long trail with twine through trees and bushes. Empty the contents of a backpack, such as a flashlight, walkie-talkie, pocketknife, spoon, sunscreen, and money, within a foot of the twine along the trail for children to find. Zigzag the twine back and forth so the trail becomes more challenging. Tape a number on each item indicating the amount of points that it is worth. Have children gather up as many items as they can in five minutes to determine who has the most points.

Sound Hike

Set up a trail system with waist-high twine attached to trees as a handrail. Blindfold the participants and start the group on one end, having each person walk though the course by holding onto the twine handrail and listening to different sounds. Leaders can play music and create other sounds for the participants to listen to as they are walking. At the end of this activity, quiz participants on what sounds they heard. A night hike can also be a great time to listen to sounds as children walk by the light of the moon. Groups should stay close together under adult supervision, and each participant should carry a flashlight and whistle.

Nature Trail

Prior to the hike, leaders can place little information labels by certain trees, rocks, and plants. As children go from sign to sign, they learn about their natural surroundings. Suggested items include a rock formation, rings on a tree stump, berries, pine cones, and animal tracks.

Cairn Hike

Cairns are trail indicators placed at junctions where a path cannot be identified, like on a rock face. Usually they are a pile of three rocks, with the largest rock on the bottom. Design a hike using only cairns to guide participants.

Program #27: Weather

Paper Wind Sock

Children can use markers to design weather symbols, such as the sun, clouds, wind, and rain on a piece of construction paper. They then fold the construction paper over and tape it to make a tube, with the designs on the outside. Have them attach paper streamers with a stapler and hang the wind sock outside. As the wind blows, the paper wind sock will blow in the direction of the wind.

Pinwheel and Wind Chime

Wind toys such as pinwheels and wind chimes are fun methods of teaching about the wind. The children can make a pinwheel with a square piece of paper as follows. With a pen, dot an "X" through a sheet of paper so that four sections are made by the "X." Then, cut from the edge of the paper toward the center, halfway along the dots in each of the four sections. Fold the four sections of paper, pin them back toward the center, and secure the folds with a straight pin. Attach the pin and the paper to a pencil's eraser. Make wind chimes by attaching fishing line to seashells, bamboo sticks, aluminum pipes, or leaf-shaped bisque ceramic items, hanging them across a wooden or metal rod. Tie twine or plastic lace to both ends of the rod and hang it from a hook.

Two-Liter Tornado

Give each child two two-liter plastic soda bottles. One bottle should be empty and the other one should be filled halfway with water, three drops of food coloring, and several small foam pellets. Have them attach the two bottle openings together with tape, closing off the openings with only a small pencil-size hole for the water to filter through from one bottle to the other. They then spin the bottles around in circles with the water end on top and watch a tornado appear and the foam pieces spin around as the water filters down to the bottom of the empty bottle.

Wind Mover Game

To teach children that wind can move large objects, have two teams of children ages six and older pretend that they are the wind and toss an exercise ball back and forth across a volleyball net or a strip of flagging rope tied between two trees. Each team has a flat queen-size bed sheet that they use to toss and catch the ball. As the team prepares to toss the ball, each team member works together to hold onto the sheet in an effort to fling the ball over the net. On the receiving side, team members hold onto the sheet in an effort to catch the ball. The teams work together against the clock to see how many times they can toss the ball back and forth in two minutes.

Sundial

Teach the children to make a sundial to teach the concept of the earth rotating around the sun. They can draw a circle in the dirt or make a circle with small stones and stand a stick up in the center of the circle. Have them take a digital picture on the hour and compare the location and direction of the shadows throughout the day.

Cloud Animal Shapes

Teach about cloud formations and how they can predict the weather. For example, stratocumulus clouds are associated with storms. If they are moving from the northwest and their bases are rising, it indicates that the storm is departing. Have children find animal shapes in the cloud formation. They can draw weather symbols seen on a weather map during the evening news to indicate a warm front (a line with triangles on top of the line) and a cold front (a line with half circles on top of the line).

Wind Transportation

Children can hang clear contact paper on a clothesline for two days to see how wind carries pollen, seeds, and air pollution through the air as indicated by the items that are stuck to the sticky side of the contact paper.

Blowing Ping-Pong Balls

Have children stand on all four sides of a table. They then move a ping-pong ball by blowing on it and not using their hands—another fun activity to teach about windstorms.

Program #28: Astronomy

Tin Can Constellations

Empty several number-10 tin cans, cut out the tops, and punch out holes on the bottom of each can in the shape of constellations. As children look through the top at the holes in the bottom, they will see a star constellation. Wrap information and pictures of the constellations around the outside of each can.

Styrofoam Solar System and Marshmallow Constellations

Teach the children to make a model solar system with painted Styrofoam balls and wire. Use pipe cleaners for Saturn's rings. Children can build their own handheld constellations by attaching marshmallows to toothpicks. The marshmallows are the stars and the toothpicks represent the lines drawn to each star to illustrate the constellation.

Learn About Greek Mythology

Children will remember more if they learn the Greek mythology and stories behind the names of the constellations. The following stories, featuring Orion, Scorpios, Hercules, Leo, Hydra, Draco, Cassiopeia, and Perseus, inspired the names of constellations.

The Great Hunter Orion—Orion is the son of Neptune, king of the deep sea, and Queen Euryale, the great huntress. Orion was such a great hunter himself that he would boast that he could kill any beast. It was a small scorpion, Scorpios that eventually killed him. Scorpios was placed on the opposite side of the sky so that Orion would be safe.

Hercules—Hercules had such tremendous strength that he killed two snakes sent by Hera to his crib when he was a baby. Later in his life, he killed Leo the lion and the Hydra, a poisonous monster that grew more heads each time Hercules cut one off. Hercules also collected golden apples from the Hesperides after killing Draco the guardian dragon.

The Queen Cassiopeia—Cassiopeia bragged that she was more beautiful than Juno. Juno was so mad that she had Neptune send a sea monster after the queen. Cassiopeia was going to give her daughter as a sacrifice to save herself from the monster, but Perseus saved the day by killing the sea monster. Perseus was rewarded for his bravery with Cassiopeia's daughter for his wife.

Phases of the Moon

The moon goes through several phases during each month. When the moon is "waxing" it is getting bigger, and when it is "waning," it is getting smaller. When the moon is "gibbous" it is larger on one side. When it is "crescent," it is smaller on one side. The cycle of the moon is as follows: full moon, waning gibbous moon, last quarter moon, waning crescent moon, new moon, waxing crescent moon, first quarter moon, waxing gibbous moon, and back to full moon. On a clear night, children can see the constellations and the moon by looking through a telescope.

Program #29: Mammals

Find an Animal Track

After they have discovered an animal track, have the children mix two parts plaster of Paris with one part water and stir the mixture until all of the lumps are gone. Bend cardboard into a tube to support the paste as it is being poured around the animal track. Do not pour directly onto the track, as it might damage it, but pour near the track and have the mixture run into the holes made by the track. Wait a half an hour and pick the cast up from the bottom to avoid cracking.

Mammals Charades

Divide the group into teams. Have participants on one team act out selected mammals without using sounds. The other teams guess what animal it is. Have the children make a list of what characteristics the mammals have in common.

Mammals Trading Cards

Create animal trading cards that have a picture of a mammal, the mammal's order and family, and similar species on each card. Also include the mammal's scientific name and habitat. Give each child a set of 25 cards with the same mammal on them.

Children can then trade their mammal card with other children to collect the complete set.

20 Mammal Questions

One participant thinks of a mammal and the other participants ask 20 "yes" or "no" questions to determine what mammal it is.

Mammal Sounds

Have two sets of cards with mammals on them. Divide the group into two teams and give each participant a card. Have the participants close their eyes and try to find the person on the other team who has their same mammal card by only using the sound that mammal makes.

Hunt for Mammal Food

Hide mammal food such as almonds, raspberries, potatoes, hard boiled eggs, carrots, walnuts, and pecans around a designated outdoor area. Participants race against each other to find as much food as they can, and then hide the food for their winter storage. Participants can only carry one item of food at a time and cannot carry or hide food in their pockets. If a participant comes across someone else's storehouse of food, they can take it. This game is survival of the fittest. The winner of the game is the mammal that gathers the most food.

Walnut Skunk

Have the children loop black and white pipe cleaners together to make a skunk's tail and glue it onto a half walnut shell painted black with a white stripe down the middle. Under adult supervision, they can use a hot glue gun to attach a black pom-pom for its head, pointed felt ears, and two small wiggle eyes.

Program #30: Birds

Cardboard Bird Feeder

Teach the children how to make a simple bird feeder. Cut a square section out of both sides of a cardboard orange juice container. Make a small round hole just below the square opening and place a wooden dowel through it. Run a piece of string through the top of the container so the feeder can hang from a tree. Fill the feeder with birdseed.

Bird Watching

Children can identify birds with a pair of binoculars and a bird field guide. Children can also sketch the birds in a notepad and receive points for spotting and recording certain birds. For example, a yellow-billed magpie may equal five points, a blue jay may earn 10 points, and a mallard duck may earn 15 points. Leaders can also purchase a feather kit from an education or nature store that will include feathers from different birds so that the children can touch and try to identify which feather belongs to which bird.

Name That Chirp

Have children listen to recorded bird sounds and name which chirp belongs to which bird. Children can also simulate duck quacks by practicing on a duck call.

Pinecone Owl

Children can make an owl by gluing two wiggle eyes and pieces of felt cloth shaped as wings, a beak, pointed ears, and feet on a small pinecone.

Birdseed Mosaic

Show the children how to glue seeds and grains on a poster board to make a birdseed mosaic of a bird. Use dried pumpkin seeds for the wings and sunflower seeds for the underbelly. Use watermelon seeds for the beak and Niger thistle seeds for the legs. Use other seeds and grains, such as cracked corn, safflower, and millet, to finish the art project.

Homemade Birdseed

With adult supervision, children can make homemade birdseed by melting one part beef suet and mixing in one part peanut butter and six parts cornmeal in a sauce pan. Children can then put the mixture in a paper-lined muffin tin to cool. The little cakes of birdseed are then set outside in bird feeders. To make hummingbird nectar, mix four parts of water to one part sugar and pour the nectar into a red hummingbird feeder. The color red attracts the birds to the feeder. Make a birdbath in a basin that is up to three inches deep with a sloped edge. Birdbaths need to be cleaned weekly with a solution that is nine parts water to one part vinegar.

Chocolate-Covered Bird Nest Treat

With adult supervision, children can make chocolate-covered bird nests by mixing a quarter-cup of butter with one cup of mini-marshmallows and melting the butter and marshmallows in a sauce pan. Then, add one cup of chow mein noodles. Pour one cup of melted chocolate chips and a half a cup of melted peanut butter chips over the mixture and stir. Spoon the mixture into a greased muffin tin to make eight bite-size nests. After the nests have cooled, add jelly beans to the nests to mimic little eggs.

Rubber Ducky Derby

Write each child's name on the bottom of a rubber duck with permanent marker. The children can race rubber ducks in a small stream to determine whose duck is the fastest.

Program #31: Trees

Sock Walk

Have children walk in socks in a wooded area for 10 minutes. Have them then look at their socks to see what collected there. Children should find seeds, weeds, dirt, sand, and twigs. Teach children how tree seeds are transported by the wind, birds, animals, and water.

Feel the Bark

Blindfold children and have them rub their hands against a tree. Have them try to guess what type of tree it is. Without using blindfolds, children can also identify samples from trees such as bark, seeds, pinecones, fruit, and leaves and try to match them to the appropriate tree.

Leaf Rubbing

Children can recreate a tree leaf. On a hard surface, place a piece of white paper over a dead leaf and rub a crayon several times on the paper. The leaf will magically appear on the paper.

Tree Cookie Necklace

Create tree cookies, which are small pieces of tree branches made by cutting the branches into half-inch-wide disks. Drill holes into the top of a tree cookie and string plastic lace through to make a necklace. Children can paint on the tree cookie and add pony beads to the necklace.

Popcorn Tree Picture

To make a picture of a lossoming fruit tree in spring, children can draw the trunk and branches and glue popped popcorn onto the tree to represent fruit blossoms.

Plant a Tree

Make arrangements with a school, park, camp, or church to plant a tree. Have children dig a hole, prepare the soil, and water the newly planted tree.

Layers of a Forest Poster

Teach children that the forest is divided into three sections: the canopy, the understory, and the forest floor. Trees make up a physical structure that many living creatures require to exist. The canopy is the home for birds and small mammals. The understory is where plants and small trees are protected from wind and harsh elements by taller trees. The forest floor is made up of decomposing leaves and wood from trees. Mammals, insects, gastropods, and fungal organisms make their home from the rotting tree materials. For a visual aid, children can glue three different colored sections of construction paper on a poster representing each of the layers. Have children cut out pictures from magazines of plants, birds, mammals, insects, gastropods, and fungal organisms that live in each layer of the forest and glue them on the poster.

Program #32: Insects, Spiders, and Butterflies

Predators Protection

Throw colored pipe cleaners onto the ground near a tree or a cluster of weeds and have children find the pipe cleaners. Teach children how bugs use camouflage for protection from predators.

Amazing Bees

Have children make a list of food items made with honey, or how people are benefited by bees. Serve children an apple or peach while teaching them that bees pollinate trees so that they are able to grow fruit.

Collecting Bugs

Children can build their own net to catch insects and butterflies by bending a wire clothes hanger around a broom stick and taping cheesecloth around the wire. Make a jar that will kill the specimen by placing two layers of cotton between two corrugated cardboard disks inside the jar and closing the lid tightly after placing the specimen in it. Secure specimens on corrugated sheets of cardboard with straight pins and display under a glass frame or place in a box.

Bug Terrarium and Ant Farm

Have the children place plants, sticks, soil, and water with insects in a glass jar or an aquarium with a screen lid. They then can observe the daily habits of insects as they adjust to their new habitat. A screened box can also be used as a bug catcher. Have the group collect bugs and make sure plenty of plant food and water is available. To make an ant farm, start by placing a smaller jar in a larger bottle with a gap in between the two containers. Fill the gap with soft dirt. Put the lid on tight and make very small air holes and a food opening that can be plugged with a stopper. Children can collect ants, including a queen ant, and watch as they build colonies. Feed them small droplets of sugar water or honey.

Preserving a Spider Web

Spray an unoccupied spider's web with three coats of hairspray and transfer it to a sheet of black construction paper while it is still wet.

Insect Racecar and Coffee Filter Butterfly

To make an insect racecar, paint over a Styrofoam ball and add pipe cleaners for the antennae and plastic wheels for racing. For coffee filter butterflies, bunch up two coffee

filters and attach them to a flat clothespin with hot glue (with adult supervision). Add pipe cleaners for the butterfly's antennae. Color the clothespin and coffee filters with markers.

Web of Appreciation

Have participants sit in a circle with one of them holding onto a multicolored yarn ball. He holds onto the end of the string and throws the ball to someone else in the circle while giving appreciation to that individual. The receiver then throws the yarn ball to another participant, forming a web of appreciation. The different colors of the yarn represent the unique contributions each person makes to the group.

Program #33: Rivers, Lakes, Ponds, Wetlands, and Streams

Big Fish Tag

One participant is the big fish, and everyone else is a little fish. The big fish tags a little fish, who then becomes a big fish. The game continues until everyone in the pond has become big fish. The last person who is tagged becomes a fisherman who then tags big fish, making them fishermen also. This game is played until all of the big fish turn into fishermen and no fish remain in the pond. This activity teaches children the need to manage natural resources.

Water Habitat

Have the children collect water in a jar from a river, pond, or stream and examine it with a magnifying glass to see living organisms.

River Rock

Discuss how rocks in a river continually move along the river bottom, becoming round and smooth as they hit other rocks in the current. Show children a river rock and have them feel its smooth texture and compare a river rock to another rock of the same size.

Build a River

Have children design a river in sand or dirt by adding water. Watch how the river flows and how it naturally forms banks by following the path of least resistance. Teach them that canyons are formed by rivers and glaciated run-off. Rivers make V-shaped canyons and glaciers make U-shaped canyons and deposit huge rocks in their paths.

Water Pollution

Pour one tablespoon of vegetable oil into a glass of water that is two-thirds full and watch the water and oil separate. The oil represents pollutants left by humans that can kill plants, birds, and fish. Children need to learn about delicate ecosystems as they enjoy rivers, ponds, and lakes.

Stream, Lake, and Wetlands Endangered Animals

Many animals are on the endangered species list due to a loss of habitat because of development or as a direct result of conflict with humans. Some examples of endangered wetland animals are green herons, leopard frogs, alligators, manatees, and giant otters. Have children draw and color pictures of these animals. Adult leaders can explain that if we are not careful, pictures will be all that is left of these animals.

Food Chain Cup Stacking Game

Children can tape pictures of animals in a food chain on four different plastic cups of different sizes, ranging from extra large to small. For example, the smallest cup can have a picture of a water skitter on it, and it is swallowed up by a larger cup that shows a rainbow trout. The rainbow trout cup is eaten up by a bigger raccoon cup. Finally, the largest cup, a cougar, is placed over the raccoon cup.

Program #34: Geology

Plate Tectonics

The earth is divided into three layers: the core, the mantle, and the crust. The core is the center of the earth and contains two parts, the inner liquid core and an outer solid core. The mantle is divided into upper and lower sections. Two types of crusts exist, basalt and oceanic. Plate tectonics explains that the lithosphere is a plate made up of the crust, the floating upper section of the mantle, and the asthenosphere, which is part of the mantle. When the asthenosphere moves, it causes these plates to move. The earth's surface is divided into 13 lithosphere plates that move. Continents rest on these plates. To illustrate this concept, float sections of foam cut out into shapes in a large plastic storage container filled with thick mud. At one time, the continents were together in the supercontinent called Pangaea. But as magma came up from the mantle, the seafloor spread, causing these plates to move. Continents were moved over time to form what the earth looks like today. As these plates collided with each other, they formed mountains on the continents.

Igneous, Sedimentary, and Metamorphic Rocks

When volcanoes erupt, magma comes up to the surface, spilling lava. As lava cools, it becomes igneous rock. Sedimentary rock is formed over time from particles of igneous rock worn down by wind and rain. Layers and layers of sand, dirt, and organic materials are pressed together, forming sedimentary rock. Metamorphic rocks are igneous or sedimentary rocks that have "morphed" into another kind of rock after experiencing tons of pressure that causes them to heat up and change.

Erosion of Igneous Rock

Place a sugar cube in a dish to represent an igneous rock. Drizzle water over the sugar cube and watch it dissolve into smaller particles. The drizzle of water represents rain and wind over a vast amount of time. The water in the dish represents a river that washes the "sugar sand" away. Eventually, the sand would form a layer that would recompress into sedimentary rock.

Make a Geological Cross-Section of Sedimentary Rock

Layers of sedimentary rock formations are formed over time and can be seen as different formations in geological cross-sections or road-cut sections. Geological cross-sections are exposed rock formations visible in areas of erosion or man-made development. Road-cut sections are the exposed rock formations that are visible when a road is cut out of a hillside. To illustrate cross-sections, have children fill clear bottles with different colors of sand. Each color can represent a different type of sedimentary rock or a geological time formation. Examples of one cross-section could include conglomerate, sandstone, siltstone, shale, and coal. Children can put a lid on the sand bottle and the layers will remain in place.

The Making of a Metamorphic Rock

Have children take red and blue clay and compact it into a larger ball of clay that becomes purple. The red clay represents igneous rock, the blue clay represents sedimentary rock, and the new purple clay represents metamorphic rock.

Program #35: Dinosaur Bones and Other Fossils

Trace Fossils

Give each child a piece of moist modeling clay and have him press it on a leaf or seashell, leaving an impression. The clay represents a lakebed or a sandbar. Take the leaf or seashell away and the trace fossil is still there. The modeling clay can dry out and harden, which represents the process of lake sediment turning to rock over time.

The Dig

Hide several small toy dinosaurs in a pile of sawdust, sand, or wood chips and have children "dig" them out using small plastic shovels and whisk brooms. Have prizes for the child who finds the most or put a number on each kind of dinosaur that represents its value.

Making and Hunting Dinosaur Fossils

Teach children to make nontoxic clay by adding one cup of flour and one half-cup of salt to a half-cup of water with five drops of food coloring. They can then knead the clay until is has the right consistency. If it is sticky, add more flour, or add more water if it is too dry. Children can put a small dinosaur toy or bone in a clay ball and let the clay dry out for a couple days. After the clay hardens, adult leaders hide the clay balls, which represent dinosaur fossils, and have the children search for the fossils. Each child should be given a small hammer and a toothbrush, to crack open the clay ball and wipe the dust away.

Make Insect Fossils

Insects were trapped in tree sap, which turned into rock-hard amber over millions of years. To make insect fossils, children can place a small plastic insect in one side of a plastic egg. Adults can pour melted paraffin wax into the egg. As the wax hardens, the plastic insect becomes fossilized. Adult leaders should never leave the children and the hot wax unattended.

Dinosaur Tracks

Use a pencil eraser and an inkpad to create dinosaur tracks on a poster board. Make different tracks that match up to different kinds of dinosaurs. Have the children guess which track belongs to which dinosaur.

Fossil Collection

Have the children collect fossils, petrified wood, seashells, and rocks in an egg carton and label each item. Rocks, such as limestone and coal, are fossil remains of seashells and plants.

Plaster of Paris Fossil Molds

Mix plaster of Paris with water and pour it into reusable rubber molds to make ammonite and trilobite fossils.

Myths and Monsters

Explain that long ago people created many myths and stories about dinosaurs to try to explain the large and mysterious bones they discovered. Stories of dragons are still part of the culture in China and Europe, where several large dinosaur findings occurred. Early civilizations created the myth of the one-eyed Cyclops monster when they came across the very large skull of a mastodon. They assumed the gaping hole in the center of the skull was an eye socket instead of the area for the tusks of the mastodon.

Program #36: Reptiles and Amphibians

Snake Game

Participants form a line by standing single file. Starting at the back of the line, the team pulls one participant at a time through each team member's legs until he reaches the front of the line. Two teams can compete with each other to see which team can "slither" all of its team members through the line first.

Leapfrog Relay

Two teams compete to see which can leapfrog over the entire team the fastest. The "jumper" leaps over one team member at a time, placing his legs on either side of his teammate as he hurdles over his hunched back, placing his hands on the person's back for an extra spring.

The Differences Between Reptiles and Amphibians

Reptiles include lizards, snakes, turtles, alligators, and crocodiles. Most reptiles have scales that cover their entire body. Amphibians include salamanders, frogs, and toads. Unlike reptiles, their bodies are moist. Most amphibians pass through a larval stage in water before becoming adults. Leaders should make arrangements for a local zoo or museum to bring reptiles or amphibians for a hands-on presentation.

The Differences Between Frogs and Toads

Frogs have smooth skin, while toads have drier skin with warts. Frogs have longer hind legs that allow them to leap and quickly escape from their enemies. Toads hop and have more trouble escaping predators. Their warts secrete a distasteful fluid that can be poisonous to some small animals, which helps the toad survive.

The Differences Between Lizards and Salamanders

Lizards are reptiles. They are covered in scales, have claws, and usually have five toes on their front feet. Salamanders are amphibians with moist bodies and no claws. A salamander's front feet have no more than four toes. Lizards are more likely to be found in the sun, but salamanders avoid the sun and require a moist habitat. Some salamanders live only in water. Children can make a table-top display illustrating the difference between the two types of animals.

Myths About Reptiles and Amphibians

Discuss the following myths about reptiles and amphibians:
- People can get warts from toads.
- Snakes are slimy.
- Salamanders are attracted to fire.
- Snakes hypnotize their prey.
- Frogs rain down from the sky.
- Snakes respond to the music of a snake charmer.

Plastic Turtle Shell

Cut a plastic one-gallon milk container in half to make a turtle shell. Children can add acrylic paint to the shell in different patterns to match different types of turtles.

Program #37: Rainy Days

Raindrop Skit

A group of children pretend they are raindrops falling through the air. Have them sit on the floor in a ball with their knees under their chins, looking happy. As the raindrops keep falling through the air, they realize that the ground is coming up fast and start to get a little nervous. Just before they hit the ground, they scream and then the children lay on their backs with their arms and legs outstretched.

Being a Rainstorm

Children can pretend that they are a rainstorm by slapping their hands on their legs to sound like the beginning of a rainstorm. Then they tap their fingers on their legs and snap their fingers as fast as they can to simulate that it is raining harder. Children can clap their hands together for a clap of thunder and then slowly slap their hands on their legs, signaling that the storm is quietly going away.

Puddle Jumping

Have children enjoy the thrill of jumping through puddles on a rainy day, always wearing the right rain gear and boots. Adults should make sure that children who don't want to get splashed are not near the puddles.

Measuring Rain

Measure the amount of precipitation a storm produces with a clear plastic container placed away from buildings and trees. Have the children chart out the daily rainfall for the period of time that the program allows.

Flood Waters

Have children set up a little town in a square or rectangular plastic storage container. They can put in dirt, clay, houses, bridges, lakes, streams, dams, cars, and trees. Simulate a flash flood by watering the town with a garden watering can and watch where the water flows. Children will learn some responsibilities of people who live downstream and the rules they should follow to prevent costly damage to their property during a flood.

Too Much Rain

The children fill a fishbowl with a layer of gravel and dirt and cover the top with a small piece of sod. They then water the sod and observe how much water reaches the gravel. To find how much water it would take to flood the fishbowl, keep track of the amount of water poured in before it floods over. Leaders can discuss with children that flooding occurs when the ground becomes saturated and the water has no other place to go.

Rainy Day Nature Quiz

Children can learn inside about nature while it is raining outside. Use the following matching game, which allows children to match nature vocabulary words to their definitions. Children can test their knowledge of words that describe the natural world. The definitions are across from the correct vocabulary word, but leaders should mix them up so that children have to draw a line from the word to the correct definition.

Vocabulary Word	Definition
Ravine	A narrow valley
Berm	A narrow path near the edge of a road
Butte	A mount
Glade	A clearing in a forest
Hillock	A small hill
Vista	A panoramic view of a landscape
Mesa	A high plateau with steep sides
Ford	A shallow place in a river
Glen	A narrow valley
Dell	A small valley
Bluff	A steep bank
Valley	Low land between hills
Chasm	A deep crack
Eddie	A little whirlpool
Gale	A very strong wind
Lee	The side of a rock or tree that provides shelter from the wind
Gorge	A deep, narrow pass
Burrow	A hole dug underground by animals
Thicket	An overgrown area of shrubs or trees
Mire	Deep mud
Knoll	A mound
Bramble	A prickly shrub
Flora	Plants in a region
Fauna	Animals in a region
Bog	A small swamp

Program #38: Nature Backpacks

Fill eight backpacks with supplies for children to take with them on a hike to explore the following nature areas: rocks and minerals, trees and plants, birds, streams and ponds, dinosaurs and fossils, spiders, butterflies and insects, reptiles and amphibians, and mammals.

Rocks and Minerals

In this backpack, include a field guide about rocks and minerals, a small hammer, a cloth bag, and a list of rocks that can be found within a short distance to collect in the bag.

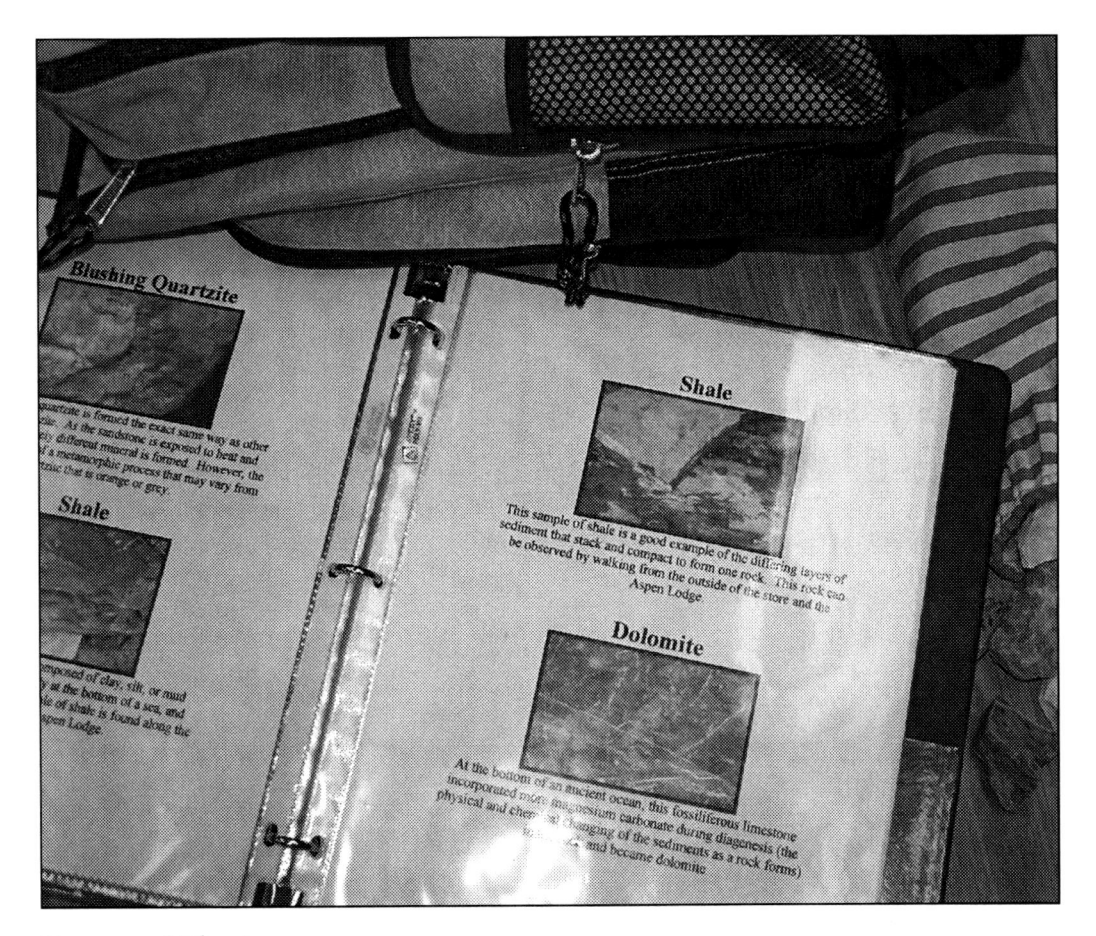

Trees and Plants

In this backpack, include a field guide about trees and plants, a stack of three-by-five index cards, and clear contact paper. Children can collect leaves of plants and trees, label them, and place them on the cards. They can then apply clear contact paper to preserve the leaf cards.

Birds

In this backpack, include a field guide about birds, a pair of binoculars, a notepad, and a sketchbook. Children can record bird sightings in the notebook and draw birds that they see in the sketchbook.

Streams and Ponds

In this backpack, include a field guide about pond life and a notepad to record all of the animals, birds, fish, and plant life they see while visiting a stream or a pond.

Dinosaurs and Fossils

In this backpack, include a book about dinosaurs and coloring pages of dinosaurs and fossils that children can color while imagining what the world looked like millions and millions of years ago.

Spiders, Butterflies, and Insects

In this backpack, include a nature guide on spiders, butterflies, and insects. Also, include a butterfly net and a bug catcher that the children can use to capture specimens for further study.

Reptiles and Amphibians

In this backpack, include a nature guide on reptiles and amphibians and information about local snakes, salamanders, toads, lizards, frogs, and turtles and their habitats so children can recognize possible reptile or amphibian habitats if they come across them on the trail.

Mammals

In this backpack, include a nature guide on mammals and a guide to mammals' scat so that children can identify what mammals live in the area by observing the droppings they leave behind.

Program #39: Gardening

Visit a Farmer's Market

Give children an opportunity to taste fresh fruit at a farmer's market, a vegetable stand, or a county fair. Provide children with an opportunity to pick their own fruit off a tree or berries off a bush.

Plant a Vegetable or Herb Garden

Children will learn the valuable lesson of "the law of the harvest" as they work in a large garden lot or in small plastic containers to nurture the soil, plant seeds, and water and weed a garden. Children will learn to reap the benefits of hard work and patience as they wait for their gardens to grow and develop.

Planting for Others

After having children plant strawberries, give each child a strawberry from a plant that someone else had planted earlier. Discuss how nineteenth-century pioneers who came across the plains of Northern America would often plant crops in the spring and leave them for other travelers to benefit from their harvest. Tell of the story of John Chapman, better known as "Johnny Appleseed," who planted thousands of apple trees at the turn of the nineteenth century that helped other families as they established homesteads on the Ohio frontier.

Water Irrigation

Children should dig trenches in the dirt with hoes and shovels to allow the water to reach the vegetables or herbs. Trenches need regular attention to clean out the weeds and rocks.

Canning and Bottling

A workshop on canning and bottling fruits and vegetables will teach children self-reliance. Have an adult teach small groups of children to bottle pears, peaches, or apricots. Children can also participate in making jams and jellies. Freezer jam is a fun and simple way that children can enjoy the taste of fresh strawberries or raspberries long after summer is over.

Food Storage

Provide an opportunity for children to learn about the importance of food storage. Children should learn why it is important to plan for a disaster by having food on hand. Grains, proteins, starches, powdered milk, fresh water, and canned foods will help sustain a family during times of personal or natural disasters.

Blue Ribbon Awards

Award children for their hard work by having a blue ribbon award ceremony, recognizing children who grew the largest zucchini, for example, or bottled the best peaches.

Program #40: Recycling

The Need to Recycle

The term "biodegradable" means that an item has the ability to break down into natural raw material elements. A child may not think about garbage after throwing it away, but the item may still exist long after his great grandchildren have died of old age. It is estimated that an aluminum soda can will last 80 to 100 years and the plastic holder that keeps the soda cans in a six pack will last for 450 years. Children should be aware that recycling provides an alternative solution to throwing away items that can be reused.

Aluminum Can or Plastic Bottle Collection Drive

Groups of children, organized by adults who provide supervision and transportation, can collect empty cans or plastic bottles from businesses with vending machines. Money that is raised can either help the children's group or provide more opportunities to recycle in the community.

Collection Sites

Children can distribute information in their neighborhoods using flyers or websites to inform people where they can find newspaper and phonebook recycle bins in their community.

Recycled Paper

With adult supervision, children can follow these directions to make their own recycled paper. Fill a blender half way with shredded, used paper. Fill the remaining portion of

the blender with warm water. Blend until it is smooth and place the pulp in a basin half filled with water and add liquid starch. Liquid starch is made by adding four tablespoons of powdered starch to one quart of cold water. Attach an old window screen to a wooden frame. Dip the screen in the basin and smooth out the pulp on the screen. Transfer the newly made paper onto a piece of felt the size of the sheet of paper and sponge off the excess water. Stack the paper, still on the felt, onto a sheet pan and put another square of felt on top of the paper. Then, press another sheet pan down on the stack to squeeze out the rest of the water. Place the paper out to dry. When the paper is dry enough, remove it from the felt squares.

Garbage Robot

Children can make garbage robots out of cleaned garbage items, such as plastic milk bottles, tin cans, and cardboard boxes. After all of the parts of the robots are glued together, the children can apply two coats of silver spray paint for a finished look.

Marble Top Made Out of Toy Pieces

Give each child a small wooden toy wheel with a wooden axle. The children can glue a marble on the top of the wheel with a hot glue gun (with appropriate supervision) and glue the wooden axle onto the other end for the handle. Children spin the handle to spin the top.

Used Clothing Drive or Garage Sale Fundraiser

Collect clothes, toys, and books, to donate to a community or church thrift store. Used clothing can also be a source of costumes for skits and plays. Children can wear used adult clothes for dress-up activities. A garage sale, in which each child brings items to sell, is a great fundraiser for a children's group. All proceeds go to further the recycling efforts in the community. The children's group can purchase recycling bins for their school, church, camp, or other organization that doesn't have a recycling program.

5

Establishing Healthy Habits Regarding Physical Activity

Program #41: Children's Olympics

Team Flag

Have teams of children make a flag representing their team. As children watch their teammates compete, they can wave their flags in support and cheer.

Seven-Foot Inflatable Ball Relay

Have children race around cones in a figure-eight formation with a large seven-foot inflatable ball. Each team should race against another team's time to determine who wins the first-place ribbon. Adults should supervise this activity because of the size of the ball. Children should not run up and land against the ball, because they may injure someone else behind the ball. The ball should not be left unattended, because the wind may blow it away. Inflatable balls can be purchased through sports catalog companies.

Kick-Off

Have a small team of children loosen their shoes a little and step up to the starting line. On the count of three, have children kick off one of their shoes. The shoe that lands the farthest wins the first-place ribbon.

Big Foam Dice Relay

Have an adult leader roll big foam dice to determine how many cones the runner has to run around to complete the race. This event is not timed, because the length of the course will vary according to each participant's roll of the dice. The fun of the activity is the anticipation of the random distance, as determined by the dice.

Balloon Trolley

Line up a team of fewer than 10 participants in single file. Place a large air-filled balloon between each participant in the line. The balloon must not be supported by the participants' hands or arms. The team has to walk through an obstacle course of cones without losing any balloons. If a balloon falls to the ground, the team has to start over. The event is timed and 25 seconds is added on every time the team has to start over.

Filling up the Bucket

Have a small team of children fill up a clean, empty garbage can by throwing 100 tennis balls as fast as they can. The winning team is determined by the time it takes to fill the can with all of the tennis balls. Each thrower has to be 10 feet away. If someone misses the can, the ball has to be thrown again from 10 feet away.

Under and Over Race

A team of children passes a small bucket of water to the front of the line while standing single file. The relay starts with the participant in the back passing the bucket over the head of the person in front of him. The second person, after receiving the bucket, passes it through the legs of the person in front of him. This alternating pattern continues until the bucket reaches the first person in line. Two teams of children can race against each other, or this event can be timed and the fastest team receives a first-place ribbon.

50-Yard Dash

Set up a starting and finish line 50 yards apart, and have children race against each other to determine the fastest runner.

Rubber Chicken Relay

In teams of four participants, have each participant run 50 yards and then hand off a baton to the next racer for the next leg of the race. For extra fun, use a rubber chicken as the baton. This event is timed. The first person to reach the finish line wins the ribbon for the team.

Foam Noodle Javelin

Have children throw a foam noodle like a javelin to see which child can throw it the farthest.

Softball Shot Put

Have the children throw a softball like a shot put, using a hoop (e.g., a Hula Hoop) to section off a ring-shaped area to stand in while throwing.

Frisbee Discus

Have children throw a Frisbee with the same technique that an athlete uses to throw a discus, and measure the distance of each throw.

Standing Jumping Contest

See how far each child can jump from a standing position and measure each jump. The child who can jump the longest distance is the winner.

Jump Rope Contest

Let children compete to see who can jump rope the longest without stopping.

Awards Ceremony

At the conclusion of the Olympics, children are awarded their first-, second-, or third-place ribbons while standing on a three-step pedestal. The middle step is for first place and the side steps are for second and third place. Take pictures of the winners and post them on a bulletin board for recognition.

Program #42: Winter Carnival

Snow Art

Mix a few drops of food coloring in water-filled plastic squeeze bottles with lids. Make several colored mixtures. Children can squeeze the contents of the bottles onto the snow to make snow art pictures with the different colors.

Snow Sled Race

Children can race down snow-covered hills in plastic or metal snow sleds. Races can also be on flat ground as children pull the sleds with rope and pretend to be snow dogs. The children pulling the sleds can wear snowshoes to help them go faster.

Snow Sculpture Contest

Have the children design snow sculptures or have a snowman-making contest. Give awards for the most creative, tallest snow structure, and least likely to melt on a warm day.

Snow Fort

Empty square, plastic baby wipe containers make great snow brick molds. Children can pack snow into these containers and stack bricks to make walls for a snow fort. For safety reasons, no roof should be added to the fort.

Snowshoeing Course

Leaders can chart a snowshoeing course by placing brightly colored plastic flags on tree branches. Participants follow the path by looking for the trees with the plastic flags. Courses should be in safe, avalanche-free areas.

Winter Survival Competition

With adult supervision, children ages 11 and older can have a fire-building contest on a metal fire plate using flint and steel and natural tinder. Place a string connecting two small poles about a foot above the metal plate. The team whose fire reaches the string and burns it in half first wins the competition.

Fox and Geese

Have a group of children stomp out a 50-foot wagon wheel–shaped playing area in the snow. All of the participants are geese except for one child, who is the fox. The fox chases the geese and tries to catch them. The center of the wheel is the hub, where one participant at a time can be safe from the person who is chasing them. When the fox catches a goose, that participant becomes the next fox. Participants need to stay within the path of the wagon wheel.

Indoor Ice Fishing Pond

Wrap white butcher paper around two long tables that are positioned side by side with a small gap in between. Cover the top of the tables as well. With a little imagination, these tables can look like a frozen lake ready for ice fishing. As the children are placing their fishing lines in the gap between the tables, adults underneath the tables attach small toys to the ends of the fishing lines.

Balloon Snowstorm

Give each participant a white air-filled balloon with his name written in marker on it. The white balloon represents a snowflake. The object of the game is for each participant to try to keep his balloon from hitting the ground using only his hands, while at the same time keeping track of the balloon.

Paper Snowball Fight

Give each participant a white sheet of paper and have him write a suggestion of other fun things that the group can do. After writing the anonymous suggestions, have children wad their paper into round balls. The group then has a paper snowball fight. At the end of the snowball fight, each participant opens a snowball and reads the suggestion out loud.

Paper Snowflake Contest

Using scissors and folded pieces of paper, children can design different patterns of paper snowflakes that are as different and unique as real snowflakes.

Sugar Cube Igloo

Children can make white frosting using one pound of powdered sugar, a half-teaspoon of cream of tartar, three egg whites, and a half-teaspoon of vanilla extract. They sift together the sugar and cream of tartar, and then whip in the egg whites and the vanilla until the frosting thickens. They can then use the frosting as mortar to make a small igloo out of sugar cubes.

Homemade Snow Globe

Children can fill an empty baby food jar with distilled white vinegar and white glitter. Have them secure the lid with electrical tape and shake the bottle to create a snowstorm.

Marshmallow Snowmen

Children can use three large marshmallows for a snowman's body and head, and use marshmallow cream to hold them together. Have them use small stick pretzels for arms and chocolate sprinkles for the eyes, mouth, and buttons. They can then cut off the end of a piece of candy corn for the nose. The snowman's hat can be a black gumdrop placed on the top of a chocolate-covered cookie. A fruit roll-up can be used for the scarf.

Program #43: Summer Carnival

Funhouse

Rent an inflatable funhouse where children can bounce, climb, and slide.

Face Painting

Children can get their faces painted by adult leaders.

Helium Balloons

During the carnival, have a clown give out helium balloons on strings.

Prizes

Purchase inexpensive prizes by the gross to be awarded to children who "win" at each of the carnival games.

Clown Picture

Prior to the carnival, leaders paint a picture of a clown on a half-sheet of plywood and build a wooden stand to support it. With the face of the clown cut out, children can stand behind the plywood panel during the carnival, sticking their heads through the cut-out section. Leaders can take pictures of the children.

Cupcake Walk

Play music while children walk in a circle, stepping on numbers secured to the floor with masking tape. When the music stops, an adult leader draws a number. When the leader states the number, the child standing on that number wins a cupcake. As soon as the music starts up again, the children continue walking around the circle until every child has a cupcake.

Cotton Candy

Rent a cotton candy machine and purchase floss, sugar, and paper cones. Another alternative is cotton candy–flavored candy sticks.

Duck Pond Game

Fill a small plastic pool with water and float 25 plastic weighted ducks in the pool. Write the word "winner" with a permanent marker on the bottom of a few ducks. Have children try to catch a duck with little aquarium nets. If they get a winning duck they receive a price.

Water Ping Pong Ball Toss

Fill a small plastic pool with water and float plastic rings with glass cups inside them. The plastic rings and glass cups can be purchased at a party supply store. Children try to throw ping pong balls into a glass cup. If the ping pong ball remains in a cup, the child receives a prize.

Dunking Booth

Rent a dunking booth and have children line up to be dunked. Adults should make sure each child can reach the bottom of the tank prior to being dunked and provide life jackets if necessary.

Bean Bag Toss

Paint a half-sheet of plywood and cut several holes out of it. Paint a number just above each hole. Children throw bean bags through the holes to receive points and win prizes for earning a high number of points.

Balloon Dart Game

With a stapler, attach several four-inch dart balloons to a large bulletin board that is leaning up against a chair. Behind each balloon is a piece a paper with a number written on it. Children age six and older can throw darts at the balloons and receive prizes for earning a high number of points.

For safety reasons, only one child should be throwing darts at a time. Children who are watching should be standing 10 feet behind the thrower. While the child is throwing the darts, adult leaders should only give one dart at a time to the thrower. In addition, adult leaders should only give the first dart to the child *after* the balloons have been set up and everyone has moved away from the target.

Ring Toss

Fill an empty banana box with several two-liter soda bottles. Children attempt to throw small rings onto the top of the soda bottles. Each child should get three turns. If a child gets a ring to land around the top of the bottle, he gets a bottle of soda as a prize.

Milk Can Toss

Stack one-pound aluminum milk bottles on top of each other and have children try to knock them over by throwing rubber baseballs. Each child should get three turns and win a prize if they are successful.

Football Passing Game

Hang a tire from a tree or playground equipment and have children throw a football through it while standing 5 to 10 feet away. Give each child five turns and award a prize to anyone who can throw it through the tire three out of five times.

Shooting Basketballs

Children win a prize if they shoot a rubber basketball through a basketball hoop or into a wooden peach basket on three out of five attempts.

Breakable Plate Baseball Throw

Children can throw rubber baseballs at thin plastic plates purchased at a carnival supply store. They should win a prize if they break one.

Pie Eating Contest

Have children compete to see who can eat a piece of pudding-filled pie the fastest. The participant who eats the entire piece of pie fastest, including the crust, is the winner.

Program #44: Night Games

The Double Agent

Pass everyone in the group a small piece of white paper. All of the papers will be blank except for one that states, "You are the double agent." After the slips of paper have been distributed, everyone scatters, trying not to be caught by the double agent. When someone is tagged by the double agent, he becomes the agent's assistant and helps tag everyone else. The last person tagged is the winner.

The Double Agent's Handshake

Participants sit in a circle on the ground in semidarkness. The double agent is determined using the same method described in The Double Agent activity. Participants hold hands in the circle and the double agent squeezes the hand of the person next to him the number of times that corresponds to the person he wants to eliminate from the game. For example, if the double agent squeezes the hand of the person on his left seven times, then the sixth person away is eliminated from the game, because the person next to the double agent squeezes the next person's hand one less time than the double agent squeezed his. The children in the circle continue to squeeze hands until they reach the targeted person. The double agent continues until someone guesses at his identity. When someone attempts to uncover the double agent, he does so at the risk of being eliminated if he is wrong.

Kick the Can

One participant counts to a high number while guarding a number-10 tin can. The other participants run and hide. After counting, this person tries to find the others. If he sees and catches a person, he jumps over the can while repeating the name of the person he just saw. If a hider is seen, but is able to kick the can before the counter is able to jump over it, then he can go hide again. If the counter reaches the can before the participant who was hiding, or is able to tag him, then that participant will count for the next round.

No Bears Are Out Tonight

One participant is the "bear" and hides while all of the other participants sing, "No bears are out tonight, Daddy shot them all last night." When the singing participants come close to where the bear is hiding, the bear lunges toward them and tries to tag them before they reach the home base, where the bear cannot reach them. Any participant the bear catches also becomes a bear until only one person is remaining. The last person is the winner, and the first person caught becomes the bear for the next game.

Sardines

One participant hides from the rest of the group as the group counts to a high number. As the seekers individually find the hiding person, they join him in his hiding space and wait until the last person finds them. The first person to find the hiding spot becomes the person who hides for the next game.

Follow the Judge

One participant is the "judge" and counts to a high number while the other participants hide behind trees, bushes, and garbage cans in a large circle. After counting, the judge has to walk around in the circle. As the judge walks around, if he sees someone hiding, he calls out his name and where he is hiding, and that participant finds a new hiding place while the judge's back is turned. If a person is caught three times, the round is over and he becomes the new judge.

Glow-in-the-Dark Frisbee

Children can play Frisbee golf in the dark using glow-in-the-dark Frisbees. Place glow sticks in tall cones to mark the flags. Line the area with several flags at different distances. Participants keep track of how many throws it takes them to reach each flag. The winner of the game is the participant who has the lowest score over the entire course.

Program #45: Outdoor Games

Human Foosball

On a large field, set up a group of children to look like a giant foosball table so that each team mirrors the formation of the opposite side. Each goalie protects a goal sectioned off by cones. The participants stand side-by-side in rows and hold hands at arm's length. Standing in front of the goalie is the first row of two participants, with their backs toward the goalie. In the second row are three participants from the other team facing the defending goalie. In the center are five participants in a row, facing the opposing team. Place a soccer ball in front of the center section, where the two teams try to kick it toward the goals. Each participant needs to stay in line formation and can only move side to side and not front or back. Adults should assist with stray balls and make sure no one is getting pulled too much as the team shifts side-to-side to kick the ball.

Jumbo Tic-Tac-Toe

Create a large square on the ground with nine sections using masking or duct tape. Participants that are "Xs" throw blue beanbags and participants that are "Os" throw red beanbags. The winner is the participant that throws three beanbags in a tic-tac-toe formation.

Parking Lot Hockey

Divide the group into two teams and play hockey with plastic hockey sticks and a tennis ball. Use cones for the goals.

Lawn Target

Arrange three different sizes of hoops (e.g., Hula Hoops) as a target by laying them on the ground with the largest hoop on the outside and the smaller hoops inside the larger hoop. Score higher points for participants who throw bean bags closer to the center of the hoop target.

Four Square

Draw a 12-foot square with sidewalk chalk and divide it into four smaller squares. A participant stands in one of the four squares. The first participant serves the ball by bouncing it in his square once and then sending it to someone else's square. As the ball is bounced in another square, that person bounces it to another square. The ball must bounce in another participant's square before it bounces a second time. If a participant hits the ball so that it lands outside another participant's square, or the ball bounces twice in his own square, he is out. When a participant is out, a new participant fills the empty square.

Swimming Pool Kickball

Have the children play a traditional game of kickball, in which the ball is rolled to a player who kicks it to the outfield and runs around three bases heading to home plate. If the opposing team hits this player with the ball, he is out. The fun of this game is the bases. Fill four small inflatable swimming pools with water to be used as first, second, and third base, and home plate. The runner has to step inside the inflatable pool to be on base. For safety reasons, children do not step into the pool until they have stopped running.

Ring Toss Football

In two teams, children toss a plastic ring to teammates, who run and try to catch the ring around their hands. As soon as a player catches the ring, he has to stop and toss the ring to another person on his team. The team tries to advance to the goal at the end of the field. The defending team tries to smack down the ring as it is being tossed. If the ring isn't caught or is knocked down, the defending team gets the ring and plays the ring where it lands on the ground and tries to advance toward their goal on the other side of the field.

Ringer

This activity is for two to six players. Give each player a minimum of three small marbles and one larger marble, which is called a "shooter" and is used to strike the smaller marbles. The game begins by drawing a two-foot circle called a ring in the dirt and placing the smaller marbles in a "T" formation inside the ring. The players cannot step inside the ring. One child at a time takes his "shooter" and tries to knock the other marbles out of the ring. If the child succeeds at hitting his opponent's marble out of the ring, he collects that marble and takes another turn. If he hits the marble but doesn't force it out of the ring, he waits his turn to try again. If he misses the marble, he takes a marble from his collection to put in the ring. The game is played until all of the marbles have been knocked out of the ring. The player with the most marbles at the end wins the game.

Water Balloon Catch

Give a team of two participants a water balloon that they toss underhand back and forth. With every successful throw, the team backs up two feet. When a team drops the balloon or it explodes, they are out of the game. The last team still playing when all of the other teams are out of the game wins.

Program #46: Dominoes

Dominoes

With five participants, mix three sets of dominoes (28 dominoes are in a set) face down and have each participant pick five dominoes so that no one else can see them. The rest of the dominoes become the draw pile. The participant who draws the highest "double" goes first and places it on the table. If no double was drawn, then the dominoes are mixed up and redrawn. The second participant tries to match his domino with the double that was placed by the first participant. The next participant can either play off of the double or try to match the end of the second domino that was played. If a participant cannot match a domino, he needs to draw from the pile until he is able to do so. If the last domino cannot be played, then the participant passes until the next turn. Dominoes are laid end to end unless they are doubles, which are laid perpendicular to the end that they match. The participant who uses up all of his dominoes first wins. If dominoes remain that cannot be used, the person with the lowest number of points wins.

Blindfolded 3-D Dominoes

You can make or purchase larger foam dominoes with dots that are indented, allowing participants who are blindfolded to feel the dots as they play. These dominoes can be purchased through a sports supply catalog.

Hand Dominoes

With a large group of people, paint each dot formation that is represented in a set of dominoes on the palm of one hand of each participant with face paint. Participants line up in the same formation that dominoes would be played out on a table.

Line up Dominoes

Stand up dominoes one in front of the other with a small space between them so they will fall and start a chain reaction. Place dominoes in patterns and in circular designs for a special effect as they fall.

Domino Trust Circle

Have a team of children form a circle, with the participants standing close together and facing the center with their arms out. The person in the middle is the "domino" and falls toward the children in the circle, with his arms folded across his chest. The children who are around the circle gently push him toward another person within the circle. The objective of this activity is trust. The person who is in the middle should develop trust toward each team member.

Human Dominoes

Participants form a circle, standing in front of each other and facing one direction. As a group, everyone simultaneously tries to sit on the knees of the person behind him without the group falling over.

6

Teaching Geography and History

Program #47: Orienteering Games

Map Reading

Teach children about map reading using a topographical map with contour lines depicting differences in elevation and slope. Have children draw contour lines over the back of their hands with face paint, putting lines closer together to illustrate the steeper parts where the knuckles are and wider apart toward the wrist where it flattens out. Teach children about map legends and the symbols used to depict items such as railroad tracks, a wooded marsh, or a picnic area.

Map Course With Flags

With orienteering flags set up in advance, teams of children can use symbols circled on a map and a clue sheet that helps them navigate toward each flag. Attached to each commercial orienteering flag is a plastic paper punch with pins that correspond to the number on the flag. The team punches the clue sheet to indicate that they have been to that flag. For example, at the fourth flag, the plastic punch will have four pins. The symbol may be a building; the clue sheet can direct the team to look for the flag on the east side of that building.

Night Map Course With Glow Sticks

Prepare a map for each group, marking certain landmarks. Participants find their way with a flashlight to designated areas that are illuminated by glow sticks in empty milk jugs. Designated areas can be marked with different symbols on the map, such as buildings, streams, roads, bridges, and dirt roads.

Compass Course

Teach children that magnetic north is more than a thousand miles away from true north, which is at the North Pole. With the help of a compass, have children take compass bearings and orient a map. Adult leaders can set up a compass course in advance in which children use pre-set coordinates and a compass and pace it off with their feet to find certain landmarks, markers, or orienteering flags.

Communicate With Mirrors

Divide children and adult leaders into two teams and give both teams a signal mirror. Send one team away to a nearby hillside or to the third floor of a building. The two teams can signal to each other with mirrors as the mirrors catch the reflection of the sun and send a bright flash.

Geocaching

Have the children go and find a cache with a GPS receiver, using GPS coordinates posted on the Internet by those hiding the cache. When the children find the cache, which is usually in a waterproof container, have them fill out the logbook. Most importantly, return the cache to the exact position where it was found.

Program #48: Hawaiian Beach Party

Children can wear Hawaiian shirts, grass skirts, beach comber hats, and plastic leis. Play Hawaiian music in the background and place Polynesian bamboo torches around the area. Make tropical banana and pineapple smoothies in a blender and serve them in a tall glass with little umbrellas.

Deep Sea Fishing

Children can cast a net over a table covered with a marine print tablecloth to fish for toys. Adults are underneath the table to attach inexpensive prizes to the net.

Balloon Volleyball Game

Fill an eight-inch balloon with air and just a little bit of water. The water gives the balloon weight. Play a volleyball game with the balloon.

Dart Coconut Game

Have the children draw a palm tree on butcher paper and attach it to a bulletin board. Attach four-inch dart balloons to the palm tree to represent coconuts. Have children who are older than six years of age stand behind a line and attempt to pop the coconut with darts.

For safety reasons, only one child should be throwing darts at a time. Children who are watching should be standing 10 feet behind the thrower. While the child is throwing the darts, adult leaders should only give one dart at a time to the thrower. In addition, adult leaders should only give the first dart to the child *after* the balloons have been set up and everyone has moved away from the target.

Wet Sponge Toss

Cut several large holes in a half-sheet of plywood for children to poke their heads through. Other children can stand behind a line and softly throw wet sponges at the children's heads. Children can paint the plywood blue and green with fish and other marine life on it.

Hula Lessons

Provide children with grass skirts and have an adult leader teach hula lessons.

Ukulele Sing-along

Have an adult play Hawaiian or campfire songs on a ukulele, and have children sing along.

Sandcastle Building

Adults can host sandcastle contests in a sandbox or a volleyball sandpit. Award prizes for the best and biggest sandcastles.

Limbo

Play the limbo song and have children do the limbo underneath a broomstick. The child who can go under the lowest setting of the stick is the winner of the limbo.

Coconut Crack

Children can attempt to crack open a coconut. After they have succeeded, have an adult leader prepare the coconut for eating so that children can taste fresh coconut.

Program #49: Jungle Adventure Day

Monkey in the Middle

In smaller teams, children toss a ball over the head of a child in the middle who is "the monkey in the middle." When the monkey catches the ball, he becomes the thrower of the ball and the player who made the errant toss becomes the monkey in the middle.

Jungle Eyes

Participants stand in a circle facing the center. On the count of three, each participant looks someone else in the eyes. If the person he is looking at is looking back at him, then they are both out. An adult leader then says, "Look down, one, two, three, look up," to start a new round. Participants have to look someone in the eyes and not at the wall or ceiling.

Jungle Animal Game

Have teams of approximately eight participants morph themselves into one jungle animal that has to move across the room. This animal cannot make any noise until the other team has guessed what animal the team has formed.

Papier-Mache Jungle Fruit

Children can make papier-mache jungle fruit by following these directions. Make papier-mache paste by mixing one part flour with two parts water until the mixture is the consistency of thick paste. Add more water or flour to thin or thicken the paste.

Continue to mix the paste to get all of the lumps out. Add a few tablespoons of salt to help prevent mold. Spread the paste on strips of newspapers over a four-inch dart balloon. After the paste dries, use acrylic paint to make exotic jungle fruit.

Tropical Fruit Basket Game

Have participants sit in a circle with one less chair than the number of participants. Label each participant as a pineapple, papaya, banana, guava, mango, or star fruit. The participant that doesn't have a chair is "it" and calls out a fruit name, and people that have that name have to change places while the participant who is "it" in the middle tries to steal a seat. If the participant who is "it" calls out "tropical fruit basket," everyone in the circle must find a new seat. As a treat after the game, adults should serve children a tropical fruit salad and include the fruit mentioned in the game.

Fruit Cereal Necklace

Give children a piece of yarn and have them string colored cereal to form a necklace on the yarn.

The Importance of the Rainforest

Using construction paper, tape, and glue, children can make a wall mural of the rainforest habitat. They should include pictures of rainforest animals, birds, insects, trees, frogs, and snakes on the mural. The following are examples of animal pictures that the children can choose: spider monkey, keel-billed toucan, dung beetle, rubber tree, strawberry poison-dart frog, and the boa constrictor. Adults can teach the importance of saving the rainforests by explaining that species of plants and animals are becoming extinct every day as rainforests are cleared for timber, farming, and development. Rainforests are beautiful natural wonders that, as humans and stewards of the earth, we cannot afford to lose.

Program #50: Exploring the Ocean

Fishing Pole Casting Game

Fill a small plastic swimming pool with water. Give each child a fishing pole with a weighted plastic fish attached on the line instead of a hook, and have them stand 20 feet from the pool. Have children try to cast the fishing line into the pool. When children make a "splash" in the pool with the plastic weight, they get a gummy worm as a prize.

Message in a Bottle

Have the children write information about themselves on a piece of paper without putting their names on it. Put each paper in a two-liter bottle and float all of the bottles in a swimming pool. Have each child swim to retrieve a bottle from the pool, read off the message, and attempt to guess who the mystery writer is. Refer to Chapter 7, Program #60 for swimming pool guidelines.

Seashell, Seashell, Who Has the Seashell?

Give one person in a large group a small seashell to hide in his hands. The group sits on the ground in a circle holding hands. A participant in the middle tries to guess who has the seashell. The seashell can move around the group. As the children are holding hands, they can pass the seashell back and forth. The trick to this game is to try to notice movement of the hands as the seashell is passed around the circle.

Bubbles

Adults blow bubbles into a small fan, which will fill the room with bubbles. Have children pretend they are fish swimming through the water. Fill a large basin with bubble-blowing solution and let children dip a small hoop (e.g., Hula Hoop) in and blow one huge bubble by waving the hoop.

Mobile of Marine Life

In this activity, children color and cut out marine life such as fish, mermaids, lighthouses, seashells, ships, seaweed, and sharks on cardstock. Children can attach the cutouts to string and attach the other end of the string to two plastic straws crisscrossing each other, thereby creating a mobile. They can then hang the mobile from the ceiling.

Seashell Challenge

Set out 20 different seashells, such as the queen conch, alphabet cone, and green abalone, on a table. Have children write the name of each shell on a piece of paper. Give an award to any child who can identify all 20 shells.

Fisherman

One person is the fisherman and chases the other participants, who are fish. When he catches them, they join hands with the fisherman to form a net of fish. As more participants are caught, the net becomes larger until it consists of 10 fish. At that point, a new net is added, with a new fisherman. The last participant caught is the winner and releases all of the fish from the nets. The first person caught becomes the fisherman for the next game.

Octopus Treat

Place eight stick pretzels into the cream filling of a chocolate sandwich cookie to make a snack that looks like an octopus.

Program #51: African Safari Expedition

Safari Shadow Animal

Children will enjoy making shadow animals in a semidark room with a lamp by a wall. Children can make shadow animals appear on the wall by placing their hands in different positions. For example, a shadow elephant is made by placing the top hand as a fist over the bottom hand with a little opening for the eye. The bottom hand is cupped, the fingers dangle down for the trunk, and the bottom thumb sticks out for the tusk.

Safari Animal Sculpture

Divide the children into two teams and give each team a plastic container full of clay. The team has to make a safari animal with clay as the other team guesses what it is.

Paper Plate Safari Animal Mask

Children can make paper plate animal masks by cutting holes in paper plates for the eyes and nose. Children can color a design with markers or paint with tempera paint. Possible designs include lions, monkeys, and elephants. To create a lion's mane, children can glue yellow yarn around the rim of the plate.

On the Prowl

In a large field, one participant is the lion, while the other participants are different animals being stalked by the lion. While the lion sits in the center of the field and counts to a high number, the other animals hide in the surrounding area with the rule that they have to be able to see the lion from their hiding spot. The lion uses a notepad to record where everyone is located as he finds each participant. The lion doesn't chase anyone; he just observes and takes notes. The lion can wander around, but should try to find each participant using trailing and tracking techniques like looking for footprints, following broken tree or bush limbs, listening carefully for breathing, or seeing someone running through tall grass. The lion should not let on that he has found anyone, but record his findings in the notepad. After 15 minutes, the lion roars, signaling for everyone to come back to the center of the field. The lion then reviews his notes of the participants he saw, and gives proof of the signs that lead to them. The last person caught, or a participant who wasn't caught at all, becomes the lion. Adult leaders should verify each child's location to support the lion's claims of where he found each participant.

Elephant's Trumpet

Let children try to trumpet like an elephant by moving their arms up like an elephant's trunk and at the same time forcefully blowing air out from closed lips. The bottom lip is tighter than the top lip, which flaps a little more to make a squealing sound.

Safari Costume Contest

Have children dress up as safari expedition explorers with pit helmets, khaki shorts, tan shirts, knee-high socks, backpacks, canteens, and binoculars. Adults can judge and award animal crackers for the best costumes.

Program #52: Japanese Samurai Night

Rice Box Activity

For an indoor activity, empty a 20-pound bag of rice in a flat plastic container and let children play in the rice like a sandbox. Sand toys work well in a rice box. Spinning water and sand wheels are especially fun.

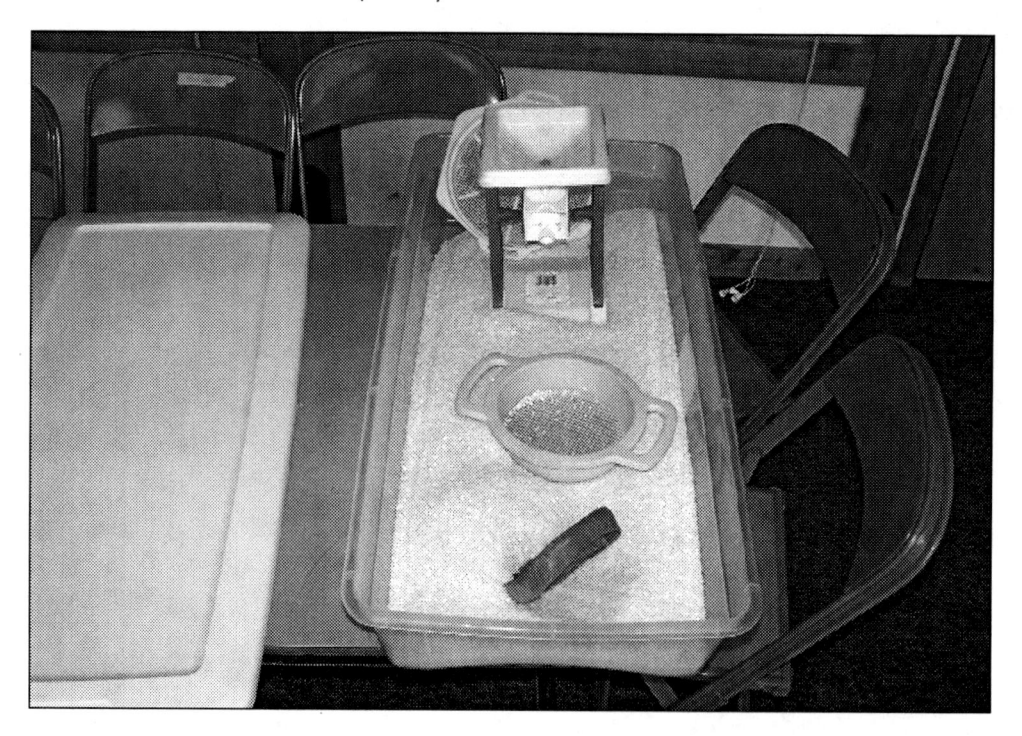

Serve Sushi

Let children taste sushi samples with a parent's permission. Leaders should have a list of children's allergies before this activity.

Origami

With special origami paper and an instruction booklet, children can fold origami paper into shapes of animals, birds, insects, flowers, dinosaurs, and fish.

Foam Sword Fighting

With foam swords either commercially purchased or made from sticks, duct tape, and heavy foam, children will enjoy the chance to learn techniques in sword fighting. Strict rules should be set up in advance and ear and eye projection should be worn.

Ceramic Pot

Children glaze greenware pots with a special under-glaze designed for pre-firing greenware and then etch Japanese writing characters with pottery tools. After this process, the pots are fired in a kiln at the low-firing cone 03. After the pots are cooled, they are sprayed by adults with two coats of ceramic sealant.

Sumo Wrestling

Rent sumo wrestling suits for children over 10 years old and adults to try a few wrestling moves. Even without the suits, children can sumo wrestle in a sandpit volleyball area with adults as referees. Boys should be paired up with boys and girls should be paired up with girls.

Chopstick Eating Contest

This game is not one of speed, but of precision. Serve teriyaki chicken, noodles, rice, and vegetables. Let children eat with chopsticks and practice their skills. Then, with a small second serving, have children receive points for every food item they successfully eat without dropping.

Kimono Lecture

Conduct a lecture about the different styles of kimonos, which are traditional Japanese dresses, such as Yukata, Furisode, Mofuku, and Uchikake. Each dress has a different tradition and meaning.

Speaking Japanese

Create the opportunity for children to learn a few words in Japanese, such as hello (ohayo gozaimasu), goodnight (oyasumi), and thank you (domo arigato).

Program #53: Swiss Day

Maypole

A maypole can either be purchased or made with an eight-foot pole, a round wooden top, a wooden stand, and 10 long fabric streamers, which are attached to the wooden top. Ten participants each hold an end of a streamer and then braid the streamers together by weaving in and out of the circle.

Climbing the Alps

Rent a portable climbing wall, supervise with certified leaders, and provide appropriate equipment. Adult leaders can also build a small bouldering wall. A small wall can be built out of wood that is about four feet tall with a slight "A" frame slant and a sturdy support frame of two-by-four wooden boards. Handholds can be placed in the studs for children to climb. Children should only be off the ground a few feet, where they wouldn't need to be harnessed and on belay. A thick layer of wood chips should be spread around the ground for extra safety. Skilled climbers could be invited to this activity and perform a demonstration for children on how to climb rope using ascenders and how to repel from a high platform or cliff.

Whittling

Children ages nine and older should be taught knife safety, including how to hold a knife, pass a knife to someone else, and whittle away from the body. Give each child a chance to whittle with a Swiss knife a hot dog stick. Roast hot dogs or marshmallows. Another whittling activity is to carve a small animal figure out of a bar of soap.

Wood Shavings Treasure Hunt

Hide several small toys in a pile of wood shavings and sawdust that children can dig through. Limit the number of toys per child. Start the activity with yodeling music playing in the background. When the music stops, start another round of hunting for toys.

Play the Swiss Clock Game

Position a small team of children in a circle that represents a Swiss clock. The child at 12 o'clock needs to rotate to the position of 6 o'clock by moving everyone in the group. The 12 o'clock child and the 6 o'clock child cannot just trade places. Everyone in the group needs to keep their feet touching those of the child on either side of them at all times and the group must move together.

Hansel and Gretel Candy House

Use graham crackers as the walls and the roof of the houses. Children can make thick frosting by using one pound of powdered sugar, a half-teaspoon of cream of tartar, three egg whites, and a half-teaspoon of vanilla extract. They must follow these directions: Sift the sugar and cream of tartar. Whip the egg whites and the vanilla until the frosting thickens. Glue the walls and roof with frosting and decorate with gumdrops, peppermint hard candy, licorice, and pretzels. Use frosting on the back of the candy to fasten it to the graham cracker structure. An adult can read the story of Hansel and Gretel out loud after all the children build their candy houses.

Wooden Mountain Climber

Adult leaders cut out a wooden figure of a climber out of a half-inch thick piece of plywood that is seven inches wide and seven inches long and drill a hole in each wooden hand on an angle. Then they cut a small one-inch wooden beam that is the width of the climber, with two holes drilled an inch from each end and one hole in the middle. Children then paint the climber with acrylic paint and follow these directions: Cut a child-size plastic jump rope in half with scissors. String each section of the jump rope through one of the climber's hands up to the small wooden beam. At each end of the jump rope, tie a knot onto the beam. The jump rope handles will dangle from the climber's hands. The wooden beam hangs from another half-piece of jump rope, which is strung through the middle hole of the beam and tied to a ceiling hook or a tree branch. As the child pulls on the jump rope in an up-and-down fashion, the hiker slowly climbs up the rope.

Program #54: Pioneer Games

Wooden Spoon and Egg Relay

Divide the group into teams and have the teams race against each other. The first member of the team runs 20 feet to a cone, turns around, and comes back, the whole time carrying a wooden spoon with a hardboiled egg in it. If the egg falls, the runner has to stop and pick it up and resume the race. As soon as the first runner returns to the team, a second participant runs the second leg of the race, and so on until each member of the team completes the run. The team that completes the race first is the winner. If an egg breaks during the course of the game, a spare egg should replace it and the runner completes his portion of the race.

Buzz Saw

Adult leaders cut a quarter-inch-thick tree disc and drill two small holes in the center like a button. Children then run string in one hole and out the other hole and tie off the ends. For part of this activity, children paint their discs with pioneer symbols, such as a wagon wheel or buffalo skull. When the paint is dried, a child then loops each end of the string around his index fingers and twists the string tight. The child then extends his hands back and forth, keeping the disc in motion. As the disc spins, it looks like a little round saw.

Potato Sack Race

Children race against each other while jumping in burlap potato sacks to cones 20 feet away and back. The first one to cross the finish line wins.

Tug-of-War

Using a 10-pound rope that is about 25-feet long, have two teams of children pull against each other on opposite ends of the rope.

Wagon Wheel Hoop Game

Children push a large a metal hoop the size and width of a bicycle wheel with a square stick that is 30 inches long and two inches square. Attached to the stick is a small piece of tin that glides against the metal as the child races behind the hoop continually pushing it. By using multiple hoops, children can race against each other. For extra fun, little wood ramps and jumps can be made.

Hoops and Graces

In this game, each child throws a round wooden hoop with ribbons tied on the hoop to another child. Each child has two thick wooden dowels in his hands to throw and catch the hoop. To throw the hoop, a child crosses the dowels, and then quickly pulls them apart, flinging the hoop in the air.

Blueberry Surprise in a Dutch Oven

Bake a can of blueberries with spice cake mix in a Dutch oven, with charcoal briquettes on the bottom and top. The juices from the blueberries will moisten the cake mix without oil or water. This blueberry crumble tastes great with vanilla ice cream.

Dipping Candles

Carefully melt enough paraffin wax to fill a six-inch metal container. To add color to the candles, melt a couple of crayons in with the paraffin wax. Children can follow these directions to make their very own candles. Cut a two-foot section of string for two 12-inch segments of string. Two candles are made at the same time. Double over the string and begin dipping both strings in the six-inch container, where the strings can be dipped and then cooled in a container of water between the dipping turns. Make sure the wax is climbing up the string; otherwise, the wax will accumulate on the bottom with no wick in it. After multiple turns, trim the bottoms of the candles with a knife, removing the extra wax that builds up. Adult leaders should never leave the children and the hot wax unattended.

Making Soap

Children can make their own soap with a soap-making kit, applying glycerin soap to color chips and scent in soap molds.

Program #55: Native American Activities

Native American Homes

For this activity, children can build models of different types of Native American homes with craft sticks, glue, and felt. Historically, many different types of homes were used by different Native Nations based on their geographical location in Northern America. On the plains, the tepee was used. In the East, longhouses were built. The Northwestern tribes used plank houses. In the Southwest, pueblos and hogans were used for homes. Wigwams, chickees, and thatched buildings were other types of homes that were built.

Warrior's Run Relay

This activity is designed for children ages 11 and older. Set up a course where participants compete with other teams in a four-person relay, using a matchstick for a baton. At the starting line, the first runner races to an archery station to shoot a few arrows in the target. After completing that task, he passes the baton to another runner, who runs a certain distance and then shoots a BB gun. A third person swims in a pool or lake the distance of a couple of pool lengths while trying to keep the match dry in his hand. The swimmer runs to the last participant who builds a fire with twigs and strikes the match to light it. Refer to the following programs when setting up these stations: Chapter 11, Program #87—BB gun and Program #89—archery; and Chapter 7, Program #60—swimming pool guidelines.

Lacrosse

Divide the group into two teams and have the teams play lacrosse. Teach them that Native American tribes invented lacrosse and that they would play other tribes in contests that sometimes lasted several weeks and covered vast distances.

Hoop and Pole Game

Have children roll a metal hoop the size of a bicycle wheel on the ground and try to throw a stick through it. This activity was a training exercise for young warriors who would use it to refine their spear-throwing skills.

Firewood Game

Instruct the children to sit in a circle on the ground. One child is blindfolded and sits in the middle near a stack of firewood. This child is the guardian of the firewood. His job is to protect the firewood from disappearing. The children around him try to take the

firewood without being touched by the guardian. The game is played until the firewood is gone or until several failed attempts are made to take the wood. A new guardian is then appointed.

Tepee Tag

Set up a large tepee without the canvas covering. Standing in the center of the tepee poles is "the hunter." This person cannot leave the center of the tepee area. Other participants are "deer" that try to run in and out of the tepee poles without getting caught. Participants who are caught become hunters. This game is played until everyone is caught, and the first person caught becomes the hunter for the next round.

Native American Crafts

Children can learn about Native American culture by making the following handicraft projects: pinch pots with clay, basket weaving from a kit, dreamcatchers, beading with seed beads, and making necklaces with stone arrowheads and plastic eagle claws.

Program #56: Fiesta Fun

Pinto-Bean Pictures

Children can arrange pinto-bean pictures of birds or animals on a sheet of cardstock with white glue.

Gold Coin Toss

Tell children that centuries ago the search for gold and the Fountain of Youth brought many people from across the ocean searching for wealth and youthful vigor. This game combines both gold and a fountain. With a small plastic birdbath container filled with water as a fountain, children toss plastic coins into the fountain from four feet away. Make sure that they make a wish first.

Hot Cinnamon Candy Eating Contest

Children can test their endurance by eating hot cinnamon candy to determine who can eat the most. Adults should set limits on this activity so no one overdoes it.

Piñata

A piñata is a favorite activity at any fiesta. After filling the piñata with candy, adults should rope-off the piñata section for safety and only have children retrieve the spilled candy after the batting stick has been laid on the ground.

Mexican Jumping Beans

Create a contest to determine how long children can stay on a pogo stick. Children should wear helmets and pads. Judging of this contest can be done in two ways: either a judge keeps track with a stopwatch or the participants count the number of bounces they make.

Mexican Hat Dance

Play the Mexican hat dance music from a mariachi band recording as children dance around a sombrero and clap their hands to the beat of the song.

Flour Tortilla Throwing Contest

Organize a throwing contest using flour tortillas as Frisbees and award prizes for the longest throw. Children can also play catch with the tortillas.

Cities and Countries

Children sit in chairs in a circle with one participant in the middle with a spray bottle full of water. This participant tries to spray another participant with water before he can name a city in Mexico or name a country in Central or South American. Examples of cities in Mexico include Mexico City, Tijuana, Cancun, and Durango. Examples of countries in Central America include Guatemala, El Salvador, Honduras, and Costa Rica. Examples of countries in South America include Peru, Brazil, Paraguay, and Bolivia.

Papier Mache Maracas

Children can make papier mache paste by mixing one part flour with two parts of water until the mixture is the consistency of thick paste. They can add more water or flour to thin or thicken the paste and continue to mix the paste to get all of the lumps out. Then, they add a few tablespoons of salt to help prevent mold. To make maracas, the children dip newspaper strips in the paste. With a paper funnel, they put rice into a large eight-inch balloon, tie the balloon, tape a cardboard toilet paper roll to the balloon, and apply wet newspapers. After the maraca has dried, children can paint designs and play their new musical instrument.

Papier-Mache Maraca

Program #57: Time Travel Excursion

Time Travel Machine

Children can make a time machine out of a large refrigerator-type cardboard box. Have them paint the outside of the box with tempera paint and add dials, buttons, and lights for special effects. Children can pretend to go back in time to meet historical people and explore strange places. Children can also pretend to bring a historical figure back to the present day. Adults can dress up as Mark Twain, Betsy Ross, Captain James Cook,

or Joan of Arc. Before these characters are introduced to the children, they can try to ask questions about each historical figure to guess who it is.

Paper Cup Time Machine

Children can pretend they are futuristic robots making a time machine by tying four strings to a rubber band. Then, in a team of four, each child holds onto the end of a string, which acts as a handle to move the rubber band. The team attempts to lift up a paper cup by pulling open the rubber band and lowering it over the cup. Once the team as successfully wrapped the rubber band around the cup, they then attempt to stack five cups on top of each other, using only the rubber band and string.

Time Machine that Zooms and Errks

Have the children sit in chairs in a circle. By turning his head to the person next to him, each child says the word "zoom," which is the sound that the time machine makes when it races forward. As each person turns his head and repeats "Zoom" to the person sitting next to him, the direction of travel will be the same throughout the circle. However, if anyone along the way says the word "Errk," the time machine goes back in time, the direction of travel flips, and children turns their heads the opposite way and say "Zoom" in that direction until someone else says "Errk." If a participant repeats "Zoom" but doesn't turn his head in the right direction, or says the word "Zerrk," he is out of the game.

Around the World in 80 Seconds

Have a race between two teams with two large puzzles of the world. The team that completes its puzzle the fastest wins the race.

Presidents of the United States Puzzle

Make two lists of all of the names of the Presidents of the United States on two pieces of cardstock. Cut the sheets into strips and have two teams of children race against each other to organize the list in chronological order, with George Washington at the top. The first team to do so wins.

Wacky Science Fiction

Rent an old black-and-white science fiction movie and turn off the sound. Have children provide the dialogue and make up new lines for the movie. This is guaranteed to be funnier than it is scary.

Program #58: Prehistoric Quest

Volcano

Have the children cover a glass soda bottle with clay to make it look like a volcano. When the clay is dry, the children paint the clay dark brown with red streaks down the sides of the volcano for lava rivers. Then, they place the volcano in a cardboard box filled with an inch of sand. They can also place small plastic dinosaurs, plastic palm trees, and other plastic plants in the sand. They fill the glass bottle with two tablespoons of white distilled vinegar, one tablespoon of baking soda, and red food coloring and watch the volcano erupt toward the dinosaurs.

Soda Pop Bottle Dinosaur

After taking the label off of a plastic green soda bottle, children can use hot glue, under adult supervision, and green pipe cleaners to make a green apatosaurus. Double-over pipe cleaners for the head and long tail and cut smaller pipe cleaner sections for the legs. Add wiggle eyes to the head.

Dinosaur Bone Gathering

Hide sticks painted as bones along a trail or in a park and have children search for dinosaur bones. Write numbers on a few of the bones and have a drawing in which the children can win prizes.

Petroglyphs

Paint a large sheet of cardboard grey and black to look like a cave wall and have the children make petroglyphs with tempera paint. Children can paint animals, people, and events on the cave wall.

Looking at the Past

Break up pottery into shards and sanitize pieces of animal bones and bury them in a pile of soft dirt. With small shovels and old toothbrushes, have the children dig for them. Children can also sift through dirt by placing the pile of dirt on a screen with a wooden frame and shaking it back and forth. The dirt will fall through the screen, leaving the artifacts behind.

Caveman and Cavewoman Life

Dress children up as cavemen and cavewomen, with white foam cut into bones for the women's hair and paper sack vests that look like animal skins for the men. Have children find small round stones and tie them with sinew to sticks to make hammers. Purchase rock arrowheads and tie them to long sticks to make arrows. Children can also grind up kernels of corn between two rocks to make corn flour.

Inventing the Wheel

This activity is divided into three stages representing the invention of the wheel.
- Stage 1: A team of eight participants needs to move a large exercise ball without it touching the ground. It has to touch every participant's elbow.
- Stage 2: The exercise ball is rolled from a starting point to a finish line in a figure-eight pattern set up by cones.
- Stage 3: Children gather 25 tennis balls and a four-by-four sheet of plywood. They then roll the plywood on the tennis balls for 15 feet.

Program #59: Traveling Through the Skies

Boomerang Activity

Boomerangs were used for hundreds of years in Australia by Aborigine hunters as a way to distract birds into nets. For this activity, children take turns throwing a boomerang in a large field with an overhand throw, keeping the boomerang at a 90-degree angle to ensure its return.

Kite Flying

Provide each child with an inexpensive kite to fly to teach them about geography and history. Kite flying started in China more than 3000 years ago. The first kites were made with China's natural resources: bamboo and silk. A kite was used by Benjamin Franklin for a scientific experiment to illustrate that thunder clouds generate electricity, which lead him to invent the lighting rod. Kites have been used to send meteorological instruments into the air to measure wind velocity, humidity, temperature, and barometric pressure. People have actually been transported in the air by kites. During World War II, kites were used as gunnery targets.

Make a Paper Diamond Kite

To make a kite, children cross two light-weight wooden dowels and secure them with string, wrapping the string tightly around the intersection of the two dowels and making a right angle. The shorter, horizontal dowel is about one-and-a-half-feet long and the longer, vertical dowel is about two-and-a-half-feet long. At both ends of the horizontal dowel and on the top of the vertical dowel, the children cut a small notch for the string that will outline the diamond pattern for the kite. The paper sail material is cut into a diamond shape, but is a little larger than the string outline so that it can be folded over the string outline and glued with white glue. They then secure kite string to the center of the wooden frame. A tail can be a three-foot piece of flagging tape tied onto the bottom of the kite.

If Kites Could Talk

As children design their kites, they can write silly messages as though the kites were talking to them. The words that children pick should be painted big enough so that they can be read from the ground by other children. If a kite could talk, what would it say? Here are a few suggestions: "How is the weather down there?" or "Now that I am up here, how am I going to get down?" or "Back off, Mr. Seagull, this is my space." Children will have fun thinking of goofy things a kite can say to them.

Civil War Hot-Air Balloon Reconnaissance Missions

During the United States' Civil War, the Union and Confederate armies used hot air balloons to spy on each other. The pilots would send telegraphs back to their troops or sketched maps of where the other army was positioned. Children can create a model of these historical events by attaching a small basket to a string tied to a helium-filled balloon. Depending on the size of the balloon, it may take several balloons to lift the basket from the ground. Children can also place a message in the basket and let another child pull down the balloon and read the message. It is not wise to let balloons sail off to litter the neighbor's yard after they finally pop in the air. For this activity, children are encouraged to keep a tight grip on their balloons the entire time.

7

Wacky Water Fun

Program #60: Swimming Pool and Waterfront Safety and Exercise

Before any pool or waterfront activity begins, it is wise for lifeguards to test each child's ability to swim. Each child should swim a couple of lengths of the pool, float, and tread water to determine what area of the pool he should play in. The pool can be divided into three areas, for nonswimmers, beginning swimmers, and swimmers. Tags indicating skill levels can be posted on the swim deck.

Life-Saving Skills

Older children should know how to save someone who is in distress in the water without putting their own lives at risk. Reaching to someone in the water from the deck to pull them to safety, or throwing a ring buoy, life jacket, or other floating item, should be considered before jumping feet-first into the water to rescue someone. To prevent a drowning, children should swim with a friend and be near that friend at all times. During swim time, a lifeguard should blow the whistle on a routine basis. Participants then grab their buddy's arm and hold it in the air as the lifeguard ensures that everyone in the pool or waterfront is accounted for.

Floating in Clothes

Children who are 11 years and older and have good swimming skills should learn to float in their clothes, which is a skill that might save their lives someday. Have children put on clothes over their swimsuits and jump in the pool feet first. Swimming in clothes is very difficult and by itself is a great skill to learn. The swimmer should take off his shirt and shoes first and then make a floatation device out of his pants. The swimmer should take off his pants and tie knots in the legs while treading water. When the legs are tied off, the waist of the pants is flung over the swimmer's head, forming an air pocket that the swimmer can trap against his chest and use to float.

Water Aerobics

Leaders can teach children water aerobics to help develop a lifelong water fitness routine.

Mile-Swim Recognition

Children can earn a mile-swim certificate or patch by swimming laps on a regular basis. Recognition by adult leaders should be provided to each child during an awards program scheduled after several children complete this challenge.

Snorkeling

With fins, a mask, and a snorkel, children can explore under the water and develop a life-long hobby. In a pool, adults can place interesting things to look at on bottom of a pool, like sunken pirate treasure. In a lake or pond, children can look for fish.

Kickboard and Foam Noodle Race

Have four children at a time race each other around floating buoys in the pool, holding kickboards or foam noodles and using only their legs. The first child to complete the course wins the race and receives a fish-shaped candy as a prize.

Program #61: Swimming Pool Games

Remote Control Boats

Set up a course in a pool or pond for racing, using floating "milk jug" buoys tied to ropes to map out the course. On the other end of each rope is a weight so that the buoys stay in one location. Boats can either race against the clock or against other boats. Provide each child with a skipper's hat while he races his boat.

River Rapids

Line up a group of 30 children in the shallow part of the pool, in two rows that face each other, with a four-foot gap in between. The gap represents a river in which the participants create rapids by splashing water with their hands. One participant at a time rides on a tube down the river rapids.

Bucket Brigade Relay

Each team lines up side-by-side and each participant uses his own eight-ounce cup to pass water from the pool to the next person, until it reaches the end of the line. The last person empties his cup into a bucket that sits on the deck of the pool. The first team to fill the bucket to the brim with water wins the relay.

The Hungry Alligator

Each team has to pick up 25 items such as coins, golf balls, or diving rings from the bottom of the pool and put them in the alligator's mouth, which is a bucket held by a member of the team. Each team races against the clock and the team that gathers all of the items the fastest wins.

The Dunked T-Shirt Relay

Up to four teams line up in the shallow end of the pool. Each team is given an extra-large wet T-shirt that each team member puts over his head. As soon as one participant puts the T-shirt on, he must take it off and pass it to the next teammate until all team members have put it on. The first team to complete this task wins the relay.

Water Basketball Free Throw

With a portable basketball backboard and rim on the deck of the pool, have teams compete with each other by throwing free throws and keeping count of the number of points each team makes in three minutes. Each member of the team must shoot the ball in this relay.

Synchronized Swimming

With a 15-minute deadline, have each team develop a synchronized-swimming routine that will be judged by a panel of judges for creativity, form, and swimming skills.

Water Four-Square

Divide the pool area into four sections and play the game of four-square with a big inflatable ball. Instead of bouncing on the ground, the ball can only bounce on the arms of a team member once in a section of the pool. Each team passes the big ball to another team.

The Great Archeological Find

The group is divided into teams of six participants. At the bottom of the pool is a golden statue of some sort. The statue has to be sinkable. Also in the pool are five other people holding hoops (e.g., Hula Hoops) that represent an underground water cave. The first person goes underwater and retrieves the statue and comes to the surface in the first hoop. That person then hands the statue to a teammate, who goes underwater and comes up in the second hoop. The rest of the team has to follow this pattern. The stopwatch stops after the sixth person finishes the task. The teams compete for the best time.

The Big Slash Contest

Children compete at the deep end of the pool to see who can make the biggest splash while going in the water feet first. A panel of judges can determine who makes the biggest splash.

Marco Polo Tag

One person has his eyes shut and his arms out and repeats the word "Marco." The other team members reply by saying "Polo." From the sound of the other participants' voices, the person with his eyes closed races toward the person closest to him, trying to reach out and tag him. The first person tagged becomes "it" for the next round.

Watermelon Pass Relay

While standing in a line in the pool, team members pass a watermelon to each other without using their hands or arms. Teams take turns passing the watermelon and compete for the fastest time.

Wiffle® Ball Relay

Dump 25 Wiffle balls in a pool. Have a team of swimmers pick them up without using their hands and arms and place them in a laundry basket that a leader is holding in the water near the deck of the pool. The team has a two-minute deadline to collect as many balls as possible. The team that can place the most Wiffle balls in the basket in two minutes wins the game.

Pool Noodle Relay

In a relay, children sit on a foam noodle and run from one point in the pool to another.

Underwater Hoop Pass

Children form a circle while holding hands in the water and pass a hoop (e.g., Hula Hoop) from one person to another without breaking the handgrip. The team that can pass the hoop around the circle the fastest wins.

Program #62: Outdoor Water Activities

Water Slide

With either a homemade slide made out of a large vinyl or plastic tarp or a commercial Slip 'n Slide®, this activity will always be a success. Children slide in a sitting position or lying on their backs. Wet the slide with a garden hose. Children should be wet prior to sliding. Placing the slide on a small grassy hill is extra fun, as long as the slide is long enough. On a hot summer day, the slide will burn the grass underneath and should be moved every 20 minutes, which also prevents creating a muddy spot where children walk back and forth around the slide.

Water Fight

Water fights are fun, as long as everyone participating wants to get wet. The safety of participants and of the facilities should be discussed before the water fight begins. Setting rules beforehand will ensure that this activity is fun and will reduce injuries. Leaders should cone off excessively wet grass areas to avoid slips. The following are just a few rules to share with your participants:

- Do not throw buckets of water at other people.
- Do not run on cement.
- Do not throw anyone in the pool.

- Make sure you are dressed for a water fight and are not wearing items that will be damaged with water, like watches, cameras, cell phones, and electronic organizers.
- Do not go into buildings with wet clothes.

A fun way to start a water fight is to give each participant a can of soda pop and have them shake it up and spray soda at each other. All of the participants will then be sticky and want to rise off in a water fight. This activity should be done on the grass.

Water Sprinkler Relay

Set up several sprinklers in a small area and divide the group into smaller teams. Each team will have one minute to collect water in paper cups to fill a bucket. The water is measured with a measuring cup and the team that can collect the most wins. Participants are not allowed to touch the hose or sprinklers. A leader that is running this activity can turn the sprinklers off and on during the course of the activity to make the water source unpredictable, as long as the amount of time with the water running is the same for each team

Leaky Cup

Divide the group into smaller teams and give each participant a plastic cup with several holes punched out of the bottom. All teams start at the same time. The team members have to fill their cups with water from one bucket and walk 15 feet to fill another bucket with water. The first team to fill the second bucket wins the relay.

Water Balloon Transport

Teams of two participants each compete at the same time. The first participant loads the second participant's arms up with as many water balloons as possible. The winner is the participant that can walk 10 feet while holding the most water balloons at the finish line.

8

The World of Music, Dance, and Drama

Program #63: Singing Opportunities

Radio Station Game

Children take turns singing their favorite songs out loud for a few seconds until another child pretends to change the radio station. When a child makes static sounds with his mouth, that child takes over singing and sings his song. After a few seconds, someone else interrupts and changes the radio station to sing their song. Each child should have a chance to sing.

Talent Show

A formal talent show provides the opportunity for children to express themselves. Talents range from music, dance, and drama to a comedy routine or a computerized slideshow presentation. Adult organizers should prepare a formal environment where presenters not only feel comfortable but also respected by the other children during their talent presentations. Children and adults who attend the show should dress up for the occasion and any audio/visual equipment that will assist the performances should be set up in advance. A master of ceremonies should conduct the show and provide a nice introduction for each child's performance. Equipment like spot lights, house sound, and microphones will give the performers the extra confidence to do their best.

Lip Sync Show

Have a concert in which all of the performers are mouthing the words to their favorite songs and performing while dressed up as the singer or band. Children can also pretend that they are playing a musical instrument. Children should sign up in advance for what type of music they will be performing. Adult leaders should screen music, lyrics, and costumes to ensure that they are appropriate for both the audience and the performers. To make the concert more entertaining, a limited number of acts in each type of music should be outlined in advance.

Karaoke

With a karaoke machine, microphone, and screen, children can sing along to music. This activity is fun either in groups or as a solo performance. Karaoke also gives confidence to even the shyest child to sing along in a group setting.

Camp Songs

Introduce the many wonderful camp songs that children will continue to sing long after this activity is over. Leaders are encouraged to include as many songs in their activities as possible. Many of the theme programs in this book will be enhanced by singing a related children's song. Adults or children who can play the piano or guitar can accompany the group as they sing. Songs like "If You're Happy and You Know It," "Waddly Acha," and "Bingo" are action songs that are perfect to start a program and get children excited. Songs like "Kum-ba-ya," "Happy Wanderer," and "Michael, Row the Boat Ashore" are quiet songs that can be sung at the end of the program to calm children down.

Program #64: Pageants

Musical Hometown Parade

Each group of children represents a parade entry and sings onstage. As a group leaves, they exit stage right and another group enters stage left, so the movement of the parade is one continuous flow. Two children are dressed up as commentators and are sitting in a booth on the stage announcing the next parade entry. To start the parade, a few children walk onstage with the United States flag and the audience stands and sings "The Star-Spangled Banner." Next, a child appears onstage as the President of the United States. He is dressed up in nice clothes and drives a plywood Model T Ford while "Hail to the Chief" plays over the sound system. After the President makes an appearance, a group of children come onstage with police hats and a plywood police car. The police group sings "America the Beautiful." Next, a little girl who is wearing a dress and a tiara and holding a convertible plywood car appears on the stage. While she is waving her hand, "Here She Comes, Miss America" is being played over the sound system. The next group of children appears onstage with a plywood fire engine and wearing baseball caps. They sing "Take Me Out to the Ballgame." The next group that comes onstage is a group of clowns riding bikes with streamers woven in their spokes and holding helium-filled balloons. While onstage, they ride around while "merry-go-round music" is playing. After the clowns, the marching band presents a musical number with hand bells. In advance, leaders color on a large poster board the musical notes to match each hand bell and then during the presentation they just point to the colored circles as the children play "Mary Had a Little Lamb" or "Twinkle, Twinkle Little Star." After the band leaves, a group of cowboys and cowgirls come onstage wearing straw cowboy hats and riding stick horses, singing "Don't Fence Me In." As the closing number, all of the children come back onstage waving United States flags singing "You're a Grand Old Flag."

Common Threads—The Making of a Blue Ribbon Quilt

A large canvas quilt is hanging on the stage. As each group arrives onstage, they bring a quilt square and place it on the quilt with Velcro® before singing their song. A narrator talks about commonalities and diversity and how common threads are just as important to making a quilt as the different fabrics are. He also explains that all kinds of backgrounds and textures can be added to a patchwork quilt and that each piece of the quilt is as beautiful and important as any another. The fabric squares cannot stand alone without combining with other squares to make a quilt. Children can sing songs from different countries or different types of music. At the conclusion of the performances, the narrator gives the finished quilt a blue ribbon.

Celebrating Historical Figures of the Nineteenth Century

A narrator describes how the many important people and events of the nineteenth century helped shape the United States. Each group will sing about these events, starting with the 1806 Lewis and Clark expedition. This group of children sings "I Love the Mountains." Another group sings about the heroes of the Civil War between 1861 and 1865 with the song "When Johnny Comes Marching Home." In 1869, the Golden Spike was driven into the last railroad tie connecting the transcontinental railroad. A group of children sings "I've Been Working on the Railroad." Another group of children sings "Down by the Banks" to commemorate the 1876 publication of Mark Twain's book *Tom Sawyer*. The last group sings "There's No Business Like Show Business" to represent Buffalo Bill's Wild West Show in 1885. For each of these songs, the children should wear period clothing. In most cases, inexpensive hats can be purchased at a party supply store.

United States Flag Performance

Each child is given a wooden square section of the flag to hold up onstage. The flag is made up of 40 square sections and stands just under 10 feet tall. The children stand on risers onstage and sing patriotic songs while displaying the flag. This flag is made from white colonial bath paneling, each approximately 24 inches square. With the white background, only the red stripes and the blue section need to be painted. The seven-inch stars are made out of white contact paper.

The flag is made up of five rows of eight squares, each painted as follows. The colors listed are from top to bottom within each row. Row 1 is the top row and row 5 is the bottom row.

Row 1	9 inches red	Row 4	3 inches white
	9 inches white		9 inches red
	3 inches red		9 inches white
			3 inches red
Row 2	6 inches red		
	9 inches white	Row 5	6 inches red
	9 inches red		9 inches white
			9 inches red
Row 3	9 inches white		
	9 inches red		
	6 inches white		

The blue section is painted on the upper-left section of the flag on three full panels and on three inches of the fourth panel. Coming down the flag, the blue section is painted on two full sections and on eight inches of the third section. The seven-inch stars are placed on the blue section. The nine rows of stars include five rows of six stars and four rows of five stars alternating back and forth, starting and ending with the rows of six stars.

Designed by Kim Roper for Bonneville Elementary

Program #65: Puppets

Plywood Theater

Cut three, four-feet-long by five-feet-wide sheets of plywood and attach them with six hinges, three on each panel. If the puppet theater is folded in a "Z" formation, it will stand by itself and fold up easily for storage. Cut a large hole for a center stage and a few smaller holes on the wings of the theater for puppets to perform in. Attach fabric with a staple gun for curtains. For a habitat puppet theater, paint on each of the plywood panels a different habitat scene. Possibilities include a farm with a barn, pig pen, dog house, and a tree. Children can play with farm animal puppets that live on the farm. Another suggestion is an underwater scene in which children can play with fish and other marine animal puppets. Other suggestions for habitat scenes are canyons, deserts, forests, and cities.

Hand Puppet

Hand puppets can be made with two pieces of felt or fake animal fur, buttons for eyes, and yarn for hair. Felt can either be glued or sewn together. Socks can be substituted for felt to make sock puppets. A third type of puppet is a paper sack puppet, on which children can design faces using markers, glue, glitter, and pipe cleaners. The ultimate hand puppet is made by drawing facial features on children's hands between the thumb and index finger with face paint. As the thumb moves up and down it forms the mouth of the hand puppet.

Marionette

Marionettes, which are puppets with strings to make the arms and legs move, can either be made from household materials or commercially purchased. A simple cardboard marionette can be made with paper fasteners, markers, craft sticks, and cardboard. Children can cut cardboard or cardstock in the shape of a boy or girl. They should cut a body first and then cut the arms and legs separately. Then, they glue the cardboard arms and legs to craft sticks and use the paper fasteners to allow movement at each of the arm and leg joints. Using markers and crayons, children can dress their puppets and put faces on them. For a three-dimensional puppet, children can use wire to attach Styrofoam balls for the body and the head and then insert crafts sticks for the arms and legs. Strings can be attached to these puppets to create movement.

Chin Puppet

Use tape to attach wiggle eyes and pom-poms to children's chins and draw on a nose with face paint. Children then lie on a table with their heads hanging upside down off the table and their heads covered with a bed sheet from the nose up. Magically, a chin creature appears with little eyes and a huge mouth. Children can sing songs or tell stories in this position.

Shoebox Theater

Children can create scenes from movies or books in empty shoeboxes by gluing in paper actors, props like trees and rocks, and set designs like buildings or a countryside. With paper actors, children can relate a story by moving the actors and props with their hands.

People Puppet

To prepare for this activity, sew a T-shirt and shorts on the front of a tarp or bed sheet. Holes are cut out of the tarp for children to put their heads, arms, and legs through. One child puts his head through the top of the shirt, a second child puts his arms through the sleeves, and a third child puts his legs through the shorts. A fun story should be told about getting ready for school. The arms try to brush the teeth, comb the hair, and maybe even put shaving cream or lipstick on. The children that are performing cannot see what they are doing because they are behind the tarp. The head doesn't know what the hands and legs are going to do next.

Finger Puppet

Children can make finger puppets of animals or people with construction paper, glue, and markers. They then wrap the figure around one finger. Another way to make a finger puppet is to make a cardboard cutout the size of the child's hand in the shape of a teddy bear or clown. With markers and construction paper, the children decorate the cardboard and then cut two holes to put their fingers through to create the puppet's legs.

Program #66: Dances

Group Dance

With the house lights still on, children can participant in group dances like the bunny hop, hokey pokey, YMCA, chicken dance, limbo, and the macarena. It is also fun to invent an original camp or school dance routine that is passed on from year to year.

'50s Sock Hop and '70s Disco

Children dress up in 1950s clothes—leather jackets, poodle skirts, and socks—to dance to Elvis Presley and Buddy Holly songs. During a 1970s disco, children can dance under the lights of a mirrored ball to "Saturday Night Fever" with their bellbottom pants and high-heel clogs.

Dance-Off

Each child has a partner that they continue to dance with nonstop throughout the one-hour-long activity. If a couple stops dancing, even when the music is changing, they are eliminated from the competition. Each couple places signs with a number on their backs for the judges to record their dance performance.

Swing or Country Dance

Instructional workshops can be given on big band swing steps or country line steps prior to a big dance so that children have the extra confidence to dance in a large group of people.

Barn Dance

Create the atmosphere of an old-fashioned barn dance, with stacks of hay to sit on and homemade root beer and watermelon. A square-dance caller can lead groups of eight children in square dancing. Several groups can dance at the same time.

Virginia Reel

The Virginia Reel is one of the oldest dances in the United States, dating back to the seventeenth century. Children form two lines that face each other, with girls on one side and boys on the other side. Two couples, each consisting of a boy and a girl—one at the front of the line and one at the back of the line—perform three parts of this dance. They first step forward and the boys bow and the girls curtsy and then they both step back into the line. Second, these same two couples step forward hand-in-hand and rotate in a circle in the middle of the line formation. Third, these same two couples step forward and do-si-do around each other, so that the boy and the girl circle each other without turning, and rotate back-to-back in front of each other with their arms folded. These two couples then form an arm bridge that the other children in the line formation dance through, each child holding hands with the person across from them as they walk under the two arm bridges. Once everyone has advanced through the arm bridges, the two couples get back in line, but with new couples at the beginning and end of the line. These two new couples start over with the bow and curtsey and the same dance process begins again.

Dance Dance Revolution™

With a computer Dance Dance Revolution program and dance pads, children can dance to the beat of the music while attempting to keep up to the dance steps generated by the computer for each song they choose.

Program #67: Impromptu Acting

Trunk of Props

Fill a footlocker with weird hats, old costumes, and odd props. Children are assigned to make a play out of what is inside the trunk. Another variation is a grab bag that children choose five items out of to make a skit. Leaders can choose whether to give children practice time for their skit or have them perform it on the spot.

Freeze Frame

Children play with one prop until the director says, "Freeze." The children then freeze in their current positions and then start acting with the prop as though they were in the middle of a scene. Props can be anything from rope or a pitcher of water to a rubber chicken or a football.

A Play From the Audience

A narrator asks for four volunteers to come onstage and then gives them a bunch of props. Without any prior rehearsal, the four volunteers act out a melodrama such as *Goldilocks and the Three Bears* while the narrator reads the story out loud. The audience members should boo, hiss, and yell during exciting parts of the story.

Stand-up Comic

Children can perform a comedy routine and tell their favorite jokes in front of other children. Children can also act out their joke as a skit. Adults should screen jokes in advance.

"... And Action"

The director yells "Action" and two actors come onstage to perform a simple task. For example, one actor named Sally pretends to make a cake by stirring an imaginary bowl. Another actor named Jerry comes on the stage and asks, "What are you doing?" Sally replies, "Making a cake." Then Jerry puts his hand in the imaginary bowl to take a handful of batter. When he gets his hand slapped by Sally, Jerry retorts with a loud, "Ouch!" Then the director shouts, "Cut!" The director complains, "I didn't like that one bit. Too slow. Speed up the action." Then Sally and Jerry start the same scene and repeat the same lines, but this time they do it faster. Both the actions and the words are done twice as fast. After they have finished with the scene, the director yells, "Cut!" Again the director complains and tells the two actors to do it like a soap opera. The two actors repeat their performance but exaggerate every line and action, with organ music playing in the background to accentuate the climax of the ending. Again the director says, "Cut," and tells them to sing it like a country western song. The two actors then sing the lines, at which point the director says, "I quit!"

Pantomime

A workshop can be presented by an actor or a drama teacher to teach children how to pantomime short tasks. Each child is then given a slip of paper with a task to pantomime to the rest of the group, such as picking up heavy barbells, being trapped in an elevator, or making a smoothie without putting the lid on the blender. After each child finishes performing, the other children must identify what task the child preformed.

Program #68: Campfire Programs

Campfire Snack—Lazy S'mores

Children spread marshmallow cream between two chocolate-covered graham crackers and enjoy.

Skits

Skits preformed for a campfire program should be done in good taste without bathroom humor or reference to death. Also, no performer should ever make an audience member perform a silly stunt in an effort to embarrass that individual. Skits should be energetic and rehearsed in advance. Consider the following skit ideas:

Hiccups—A man and his wife drive up to a drugstore and the man walks in, leaving his wife in the car. He asks the pharmacist how to cure hiccups that have lasted for days. The pharmacist replies excitedly that he knows just the thing. He turns around, puts on a monster mask and jumps up and down yelling at the customer. When taking off the mask, the pharmacist inquires if that did the trick. The very frightened customer tells the pharmacist that he will check with his wife in the car to see if her hiccups are gone.

Invisible Bench—One girl pretends that she is sitting on an invisible bench. A boy walks on the stage and asks what she is doing. The girl tells him that she is sitting on an invisible bench, so he sits down. Over the next few moments several children ask what is going on and are told about the invisible bench, and then sit down as well. Finally,

a girl comes on the stage and after being told about the invisible bench, says "Oh, that old invisible bench, it was broken so I threw it away." With this news, all of the children on the invisible bench fall to the ground.

No Fish Under This Ice—A father takes his young son out to enjoy a day of ice fishing. The boy is so proud of his dad for teaching him about nature that he is listening eagerly to his father boast about how much he knows. They start to make a hole in the ice when a woman's voice is heard, stating emphatically, "There are no fish under this ice." The father and his son move a few feet away, but the voice repeats the same thing. "Wow, Dad, is that Mother Nature guiding us to where the fish are?" Then the voice is heard yelling, "No, I am the ice rink manager, and there are no fish under this ice!"

Run-Ons

Run-ons are shorter than skits. The children run on and say something and then run off the stage. One example is called Light Snack, in which one child has a flashlight held up next to his mouth. Someone else asks, "What are you doing?" The person with the flashlight replies, "Having a light snack!"

Program #69: Slideshows

Slideshow of Children's Programs

A computerized slideshow with pictures taken with a digital camera is a convenient way to present to parents and children the fun activities done with the different age groups. Slideshow programs can be set to either fast-paced or reflective music. Pictures can be burned onto a CD and given as a keepsake or posted on the organization's website for children to enjoy later.

Photography Workshop

Children can be in charge of taking pictures of the activities they were involved in during the day- or week-long program, either with a digital camera or a 35 mm camera. Nondigital photos can be scanned into a computer. A workshop in which photography skills are taught will provide children confidence and practice to take quality pictures. Awards for the most outstanding pictures can be given to the children after the slideshow presentation.

Creating a Slideshow

Children can help create and edit the slideshow or help by voting on the slides to put in the final show. They can assist with the music, timing of the slides, and how transitions are made from one slide to the next.

Tributes

As part of a pageant, children can create a tribute to a place or a person. For example, in a patriotic pageant, a slideshow could capture beautiful images of America's national parks while "This Land is Your Land" is playing in the background. If children are working with each other during a day- or week-long program, a slideshow can pay tribute to "unsung heroes." These children can be recognized for their service to others or their help to leaders in preparing for an activity or in its cleanup. This type of recognition will make a difference in the lives of these children.

The Slideshow Game

Two children hold up a king-size flat sheet while standing on stepladders. The sheet represents a slideshow screen, but it is actually a curtain the children can use to act out each snapshot. In a hat are several slips of paper, each with a different snapshot description. One child picks out a slip and reads the description, describing a snapshot while several children behind the bed sheet pose in that position. For example, one description can be of a picture of a family picnic near an anthill. A red ant just bit Junior, and grandma dropped the chocolate fudge cake on the dog because the dog ran through her legs chasing after a squirrel. After each scene, someone yells, "Click," the bed sheet goes up, and a new slip of paper is read. The actors behind the sheet only have a few seconds to prepare before the sheet is dropped and they are in a new snapshot scene.

Silent Western Movie

Children can create a "silent western movie" slideshow by taking black and white photos with a digital camera. They should create computer text slides that have written dialogue for each scene, such as "Oh, Chester, the foxes are in the chicken coop again." Children pose with exaggerated facial expressions, and old-fashioned organ music will give the movie its emotional feel.

9

Developing Talents and Skills in Arts and Crafts

Program #70: Art Projects

Sand Picture

Sand picture art boards can be purchased through children's art-supply catalogs. Each child is given an art board. After removing the protective covering, children place colored sand on the sectioned-off sticky surfaces of the art board. Like a paint-by-numbers art set, each sectioned area requires a different color. When the children apply different colors of sand to each section, pictures of cats, dinosaurs, racecars, etc., will begin to appear.

Window Mural

Children can design a mural in their classroom window with tempera paint. Children should paint on the inside of the window, not on the outside where the paint would be exposed to rain.

Foil Art

Children can rub a thin layer of copper foil over plastic picture molds and then fill in the details with a sharp wooden dowel. Pictures could include a pirate ship, lions, cowboys, or trains.

Tissue Art

Children glue colored two-inch squares of tissue paper to create an outline of an animal, car, or tree on a piece of cardstock.

Shrink Art

Have children design shrink art with special plastic that can be purchased at craft stores. Children draw animals, butterflies, dinosaurs, or flowers with permanent markers and cut them out with scissors. The shrink-art plastic is placed on an aluminum cookie sheet and baked for two minutes in a preheated electric oven set at 250 degrees Fahrenheit. Adults should watch the shrink art in case the item shrinks to the desired size before the timer on the oven goes off.

Painting With Sponges

Children can create fun images using tempera paint and precut sponges to make pictures of animals, bugs, or fish on paper.

T-Shirt Design and Cardboard Puzzle

Children can use fabric paint or markers to create their own designs on T-shirts. Children can also make puzzle pictures with precut blank cardboard puzzles that they color with markers.

Self-Portrait

Make an outline of a child with sidewalk chalk and have him fill in the facial features and clothes to make a self-portrait.

Velvet Picture

Purchase velvet pictures at craft stores and have the children color around the velvet borders to create colorful pictures.

Paperclip Necklace

Children can connect paperclips together to form a necklace. Using decorative vinyl contact paper that is cut into strips, children wrap the adhesive end around each paperclip.

Program #71: Painting Techniques for Bisque Ceramics

Children must be nine years of age and older to participate in the following painting projects.

Antiquing

After applying acrylic paint to ceramic bisque, children dab a dark coat of antique gel and distribute it equally with a brush, wiping off the excess with a cloth. The antiquing process will cover up any gaps children missed when painting and fill in some of the crevasses in the project, giving the item a more finished look. After the antiquing process, adults spray the ceramic piece with a ceramic sealant.

Dry Brushing

After the acrylic paint has dried on a bisque item, children can dry brush over the details to give the piece a softer look. The dry-brush technique entails using paint that is still left in a brush that is basically dry to the touch. This technique adds a soft highlight of color to an already painted project. After dry brushing, adults spray the ceramic piece with a ceramic sealant.

Chalking

As an alternative to painting bisque with acrylic paint, children can apply colored chalk to their projects. Adults then spray with a ceramic sealant to keep the chalk from smearing.

Crackling

This technique will crack the topcoat of the acrylic paint on the bisque item to make the paint look old. To start, children apply a dark color of acrylic paint on a bisque item like a ceramic buffalo skull or vase. The paint should be dry before the children add the crackle gel. They must allow the crackle gel to dry long enough to be tacky before adding a topcoat of a light-colored acrylic paint. Children can thin out the paint for the topcoat with a couple of drops of water and apply in one direction.

Marble Round Vase

Children can pour white acrylic paint with a sheen finish into a round pool on a square piece of aluminum foil. They should pick out two other colors that will form a contrast when marbled together. Children should pour these two contrasting colors on opposite sides on the aluminum-foil square next to the pool of the white paint. With a small stick, they run two zigzag patterns through the paints, one going vertical and the other going horizontal. They then roll the vase in the paints. They should turn the finished product upside down to dry on a pencil that is stuck in a brick of Styrofoam.

Marble Pillow Vase

With adult supervision, children can apply two thin coats of acrylic paint to the bisque vase and spray with a porcelain sealant. Have them place a candle on the table, as a second person holds the vase and rotates it above the candle. The first person takes a stainless steel knife and divides the flame, causing smoke to adhere onto the vase. After the marbling is complete, adults should spray the vase twice with the porcelain sealant.

Program #72: Glazing Techniques for Bisque Ceramics

Children must be nine years of age and older to participate in the following glazing projects.

Underglazes

Using bisque ceramic tiles, have children paint a picture with underglazes, which allow the child to paint multiple colors on the tile more easily than when using regular glazes. Then, fire the tiles in a tile setter at a 06-firing cone.

Bubble Glazing

Under adult supervision, children apply three coats of a light-colored nontoxic glaze to a bisque vase. They should mix four teaspoons of underglaze, three teaspoons of water, and several drops of non-degreaser dish soap. Children blow through a straw into this mixture, forming bubbles all around the vase. The bubbles should pop on their own so that the glaze doesn't smear on the vase. Once the vase is covered with bubbles, the children should mix another glaze with water and dish soap for a contrast color. After the vase has a second coat of bubbles, fire the vase at a 06-firing cone.

Marble vase, glazed bubble vase, and multicolored marble vase

Marble Glaze Vase

With adult supervision, children can participate in this project by applying three coats of clear overglaze to a bisque vase and then fire it at a 06-firing cone. After the vase has cooled, adults can spray each vase with two coats of a porcelain sealant to give the vase a matte look. Then, each child places a candle on the table and, with the help of a second person, each child can hold the vase and rotate it above the candle. The second person takes a stainless steel knife and divides the flame, causing smoke to adhere onto the vase. After the marbling is complete, adults should spray the vase once with a porcelain sealant.

Decals

Children start by glazing and firing the bisque item in a light color, applying three coats of clear overglaze. After the project is cooled and the surface is clean, a decal can be applied. They should place the decal in a bowl of warm water, completely submerging it to remove the paper attached to the back. Remind the children to put only one decal in the water at a time. The decal will curl at first and then begin to lay flat again. After the decal has been in the water for one minute, children can check to see if the decal moves on the paper. If the decal moves, it is ready to be fastened on the project. Holding the decal in the center with one finger, children should press the air bubbles with the other fingers. Air bubbles should be removed by pressing from the center to the edges. After the project has dried for three hours, they can wipe off any excess glue around the decal before firing in a kiln for three hours at a 016-firing cone.

Mystery Glaze

Have children apply a nontoxic glaze on a bisque item such as a frog, dragon, lizard, or snake so that they do not know what color it will be when it comes out of the kiln. Because frogs, dragons, lizards, and snakes can be many different colors, children will be surprised when the final project is finished.

Porcelain Finish on Glazed Ceramics

After firing a ceramic item that has been glazed with a clear gloss glaze at a 06-firing cone in a kiln, adults can spray a porcelain sealant over the item to give it a softer porcelain finish.

Program #73: Crafts

Plastic Lace Braiding (Boondoggle)

Children nine years of age and older will enjoy braiding plastic lace key chains by attaching two strands of different-colored lace to a lanyard hook and looping one colored strand over and under the other colored strand, which is looped, and pulling the lace tight each time to form a checkerboard pattern.

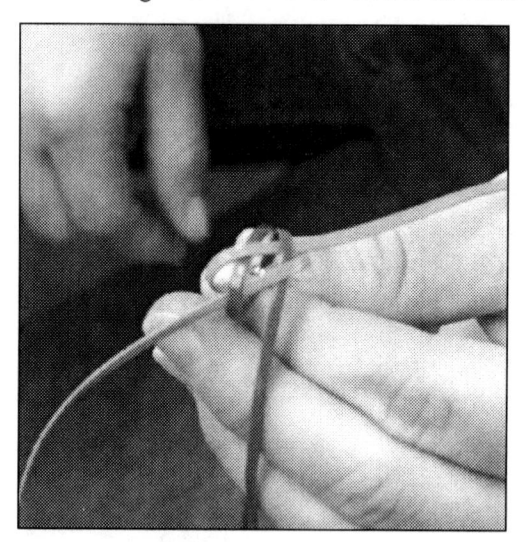 

Plastic or Foam Visor

Purchase inexpensive plastic or foam visors from a craft supply store and let children personalize their visor by applying glitter and foam shapes, or by coloring them with permanent markers.

Wooden Animals Magnet

With craft sticks and precut wooden shapes, children can use washable markers and glue to design animal shapes and then apply adhesive magnetic tape to the back.

Collage Frame

On wooden or cardboard frames, children glue assorted macaroni shapes, which can be painted individually with acrylic paint for a colorful frame. Or, the macaroni can be spray painted with either gold or silver spray paint.

Ojo De Dios

Children cross two craft sticks together and lash them together. Then, they weave different layers of yarn or string in and out to completely wrap it around the craft stick and form a multilayered yarn diamond.

Wooden Yo-Yo

Purchase wooden yo-yo kits at a craft store for the children to assemble and paint with acrylic paint. A yo-yo contest can be held to determine who has the fanciest tricks. The winner of this contest receives another yo-yo to make.

Seashell People

With adult supervision, children can design wacky people with seashells and wiggle eyes by using a hot glue gun. Pipe cleaners can be attached for the arms and legs.

Yarn Art

Children make designs out of yarn strips and a square section of cardboard. They can start by making a pattern with white glue on the cardboard and draping yarn over the glue. When the glue has dried, the yarn art can be displayed on the wall.

Eyeball Glasses

With adult supervision, children can use a hot glue gun to attach several wiggle eyes to a cheap pair of glasses.

Egg Carton Caterpillar

With adult supervision, children can cut up cardboard egg cartons and make a caterpillar by using a hot glue gun to connect five different egg carton sections. They can then add some fun features to the caterpillar like wiggle eyes, sequins, feathers, glitter, and pipe cleaners.

Tape and Shoe Polish Bottle

Children can cover the outside of an empty steak sauce bottle with little pieces of masking tape and then cover the tape with brown shoe polish, wiping off the excess shoe polish.

Program #74: Leatherwork

Leatherwork crafts are recommended for children nine years of age and older.

Leather Stamping Tools

Children can dampen a leather item with a wet sponge and pound a leather tool with a wooden mallet. Each stamping tool has a different design pattern, letter of the alphabet, or pictorial stamp. As children strike the mallet to the stamping tool, they should have a steady hand that will make crisp and deep impressions. Both the wrist and the hand should be used when striking down on the mallet. A leather press allows children to insert a stamp and press down on the lever to make perfect stamp impressions every time. Inexpensive round leather coasters are an easy start for children to practice their leatherwork skills. On these coasters, children make several stamp impressions and use a leather hole punch to make a hole. They can then loop plastic lace through for a leather necklace by adding pony beads and plastic bear claws.

Setting Belt Snaps

Many belts come with snaps already set in the belt, but this is another leatherworking skill that children can learn. To set a belt snap, children place the snap-setting anvil underneath the leather belt with the back side of the belt facing up. The cap of the snap rests on the anvil underneath the belt. The cap will show on the front side of the belt and the socket will be on the back. The socket is on top of the belt, lined up to the cap. The snap socket setter tool is held by the child, who strikes it with a mallet to attach the socket to the cap.

Staining

Stains, dyes, and paints can be applied after designs have been pressed into the dry leather. Children can apply stains and dyes with a wool dauber wearing latex gloves. Acrylic paints can be applied with brushes and be thinned out with water for softer tones. After the stain and paint have dried, children should apply two coats of sheen finish. The first coat needs to be applied with a damp sponge deep into the cuts and impressions of the leather. For a natural look, children just apply the sheen finish without staining or painting.

Lacing

Projects that use plastic or leather lacing require techniques for attaching two pieces of leather together, such as the whipstitch, double loop, or running stitch. Children can practice these lacing techniques while making projects such as coin purses, wallets, key cases, knife pouches, key fobs, moccasins, and leather vests.

Leather Crafts

Other leather crafts include a toy leather tomahawk, mini leather tepee, toy leather canoe, and a piece of leather stretched out with sinew over a wooden frame to display camp patches. Leather wristbands that snap together can be stamped, tooled, and stained. Suede leather lace wristbands can be braided and snapped together. Hair barrettes and bolo ties can also be made with leather.

Program #75: Beads

Crafts involving beads are recommended for children seven years of age and older.

Pony Bead Bandanna

Children can cut several half-inch strips into a cloth bandanna, two inches deep along the border of the fabric. They then attach different-colored pony beads to the cloth strips and tie off each strip. When the child wears the bandanna, a beadwork design hangs off the edge of the bandanna.

Beaded Key Ring and Alphabet Beaded Bracelet

With beads that are sport balls, animal shapes, stars, hearts, or even skeleton heads, children can decorate plastic lace dangling from a one-inch key ring. For bracelets, children can string alphabet beads to spell their names.

Wooden Bead People

Twisting pipe cleaners to form a body with arms and legs, children can use large wooden beads and spools for the torso and head. Smaller wooden beads and spools can be strung on the arms and legs. Children then add a face with a fine-tip permanent marker.

Hawaiian Lei

Children can cut out construction paper flowers and punch holes through the center with a paper punch. They then can string the paper flowers with straw beads and yarn in between each flower to form a lei.

Glass and Wooden Bead Necklace

Children string several gemstones and glass, ceramic, wooden, or metallic beads with fishing line to make beaded necklaces. They can then attach lobster clasps to both ends of the fishing line.

Beaded Lizard

Children can make a beaded lizard with four feet of plastic lace, 28 green pony beads, and 18 yellow pony beads by following these directions. Start by threading one yellow bead for the nose. For the second row, place two green beads for the brow and cross over the lace in opposite directions. Pull the lace, tightly forming a loop with one bead on top of the two beads that are underneath with the lace crossed over. The eyes are next, with two yellow beads separated by a green bead. Again the lace is threaded through the beads going in opposite directions. The neck is formed with two green beads followed by three green beads for the shoulders. At the shoulders, make a loop for three green beads that will represent arms on both sides of the body. The hands and feet will be three yellow beads each. The body will have three rows of four beads, with a loop of three green beads for the legs. For the tail, start with three beads, then two beads, and then six rows of one bead per row to end the tail. Use both green and yellow beads for the tail.

Program #76: Pottery

Children 10 years of age and older can make wonderful pieces of pottery by using their imagination to create such pieces as bowls, plates, cups, and vases. This program focuses on teaching children the basics of pottery. It is up to the children to turn these techniques into works of art.

Wedging the Clay

Using MCW 90 grey clay, children should wedge the clay to make it more pliable and easier to work with. It also helps to compress the clay to get any air bubbles out. Children wedge the clay by folding it over and pressing down on it, and then kneading it somewhat like dough. They should always be careful not to fold air bubbles into the clay when wedging it.

Pottery Wheel and the Initial Stage of Throwing

After wetting the pottery wheel with a sponge, children should literally slam the clay onto the wheel as close to the center as possible, giving it a secure hold. They should then turn the wheel to the fastest speed by stepping on the pedal. The toe of the foot

pedal makes the wheel goes faster and the heel of the foot pedal allows the wheel to go slower. Electric wheels stay at a constant speed. Children should wet their hands before starting and place the heel of one hand up against the clay. The arm should be braced against the body for extra strength for the hand to move the clay around. The bottom of the hand should be kept against the wheel so the clay doesn't move out at the bottom. When the clay becomes tall and skinny, the child should use his other hand to push the clay down into the wheel. The pot will be thrown off-center again because of air bubbles or lumps in the clay. The child can re-center the clay in its flat state by bringing it up and in.

Opening up the Pot

The child needs to steady his arm against the splash plate, find the center of the clay with a finger, and press down to make a hole. The hole should be about a quarter-inch from the bottom, leaving enough clay to support the bottom of the pot. The next step is for the child to hold one side of the pot and put a finger of his other hand into the hole to move the clay sideways. This step should be done until the walls of the pot are about a half-inch thick.

Design the Pot

Remind the children to keep the top of the pot thinner than the bottom, leaving the bottom thicker for strength. To make the pot taller, the child should place his hands on the sides of the pot while moving his hands up the pot. To widen the pot into a bowl, the child should place one of his hands inside and the other hand outside. The outside hand is used as a guide, while the inside hand pushes gently to make the desired shape of the bowl. Designing bands in the pot is accomplished by holding a wooden pottery tool steady against the side of the pot and using a small sponge to wipe off the excess clay.

Removing the Pot From the Wheel

The child needs to wipe off the splash plate with a large sponge. Then, he can remove the pot by using wire. He must use both hands so that his thumbs can press down against the wheel and pull back the wire through the bottom of the pot. The child should move the pot onto a board, which should also be wet. When the pot is on the board, the child should carefully remove the wire and let the pot dry for three weeks before firing it in a kiln, at the low 03-firing cone.

Program #77: Painting and Drawing

Primary Colors

Teach children about the primary colors and secondary colors by having each child mix the primary colors with acrylic paint on a paper plate to make secondary colors.

Paper Plate Spin Art

Poke a pencil through a paper plate and have children squirt nontoxic tempera washable paint onto the paper plate as it spins. Children will also learn about mixing colors and abstract art.

Water Coloring

Give each child a sheet of cold-press water coloring paper and a set of eight washable watercolors. Have the children paint a landscape scene with watercolors.

Oil Pastels

Using oil pastels, children can create a picture of a vase of flowers that is sitting in front of them. Have them focus on soft tones.

Colored Pencils

With a mirror by their side, have the children create self-portraits using colored pencils.

Charcoal Pencils

Teach children about texture and light as they charcoal a still life, like a round ball, a square box, and a pyramid shape. Place a lamp on one side of the object, so that children can charcoal the contrast of the light and shadows.

Wooden Mannequin

Have children draw a picture of a person by using a wooden mannequin model to learn about the contours of the human form. They should place the model in different positions for multiple drawings.

Animation Flip Book

Give children a notepad in which they can make a cartoon flip book by drawing the same cartoon character in a scene on every page, with slight differences to the character from page to page. When the child is finished, he can flip through the book with his thumb and watch the cartoon character move around on paper.

Crayon Scratch Art

Have children cut a poster board into two sections. On the first section, have each child color a large design with crayons and paint over the entire design with black tempera paint. On the second section of poster board, have the children cut out small designs such as stars, planets, the sun, or the moon and place them on the black poster board with a paperweight on each cut-out. Children then scratch off the black paint, except where the cut-outs are. After a child has scratched to the crayon surface, have him remove the cut-outs, exposing the black shapes against the crayon design.

Program #78: Scrapbooks

With the necessary tools before them, children can design creative scrapbook pages. This program outlines resources available for children.

Scrapbook tools include nontoxic glue sticks, regular scissors, scissors with different patterns (inchworm, scallop, royal, jigsaw, or ripple), rulers, fine tip permanent makers, acid-free pens, paper crimpers, and paper cutters. Tools and materials used for scrapbook pages can also be used to make homemade greeting cards.

Main Background Page

A theme-based background paper, which should be acid-free, will serve as the starting point for scrapbooking. Sheets can represent a theme such as the outdoors, sports, dinosaurs, maps, butterflies, or flowers.

Pictures

Adult leaders can print pictures of the children that were taken during other programs. Children can place their photos for their scrapbooking page on a half-sheet of acid-free colored paper for a border that is glued onto the main scrapbook page.

Paper Die-Cuts and Crimping

Children can make their own paper die-cuts with a die-cutting machine, or leaders can purchase die-cuts and include them in a kit. Die-cuts come in many varieties and can represent almost any theme. With a paper crimper, children make a "wrinkle" design with paper to add to the design of the scrapbook page.

Stamps, Craft Punches, and Stickers

Hundreds of stamp designs are available for children to choose from. They simply apply ink from an inkpad and press the stamp onto the scrapbook page. In addition to die-cuts, stickers can be placed on the main page and tied into the theme. Small craft punches with different shapes can also give the scrapbook page a unique look. Punches come in many difference shapes and sizes, such as pine trees, chili peppers, music notes, and seahorses.

Embossing

Using ink with pigment to make the stamp impression, children then lightly apply the embossing powder while the ink is still wet and shake off the extra powder. Adults should supervise while children add heat by holding an iron near the paper without putting the iron directly on the paper.

Borders and Silk Flowers

Children can glue ribbons or hemp to make exciting designs and borders on a page or snapshot. With adult supervision, flat silk flowers can be hot-glued to the page, adding a three-dimensional texture to the project.

Page Protectors

Page protectors serve two functions for scrapbook workshops. In addition to protecting the final scrapbook page, they serve as an envelope for the materials for scrapbook kits.

10

Increasing Citizenship

Program #79: Trail of Heroes

Make 15 wooden signs, each with a picture and a short biographical sketch of a well-known hero. Place the signs on a trail with approximately 10 yards between them. Have an adult leader stand by each sign prepared to talk about the contribution and the positive example of each hero. Heroes can be sports figures, political leaders (local, national, or world leaders), inventors, religious leaders, or historical figures. Divide the children into small teams and have an adult leader guide them blindfolded from sign to sign. As each team arrives at each sign, the children take off their blindfolds and listen to the presentation. At the end of the trail of heroes, children meet in an outdoor amphitheater or lodge for the finale. A local athlete, soldier, firefighter, or police officer can give a short talk about setting goals and working toward dreams. Children are then organized back into their teams to develop their own "Hall of Heroes," which is a list of meaningful people in their lives.

Hall of Heroes

Children are given a form to identify their personal heroes and explain how they can be an example to someone else. Once this questionnaire is given to each child, they should spend some time filling out the answers to the following questions to create their own "Hall of Heroes":

- List five of your heroes.
- What have they done to become heroes to you?
- What have you learned from them?
- What characteristics do they have that you try to emulate?
- What can you do to be a hero for someone else?
- What are your strengths so that you can be an example to someone else?
- Think of five people in your life that you can be a hero to.

Pictures and Stories

Have an adult leader relate to each team who his heroes are, share pictures of his heroes, and tell stories about them. The leader can encourage each child to collect a picture of his hero along with a meaningful story about how his hero demonstrated a positive example.

Letter of Appreciation

Whenever feasible, encourage children to write a letter of appreciation to their heroes for making a difference in their lives. When the hero is a stranger to the child, it is wise for adult leaders to collect the letter and mail it with a cover letter from the organization explaining the activity. All future correspondence should go through the organization's address.

Program #80: Service Projects

Scavenger Hunt Food Drive

Organize the children into smaller teams with an adult leader assigned to each team. Give them a list of items to collect, each with an assigned point value. For example, sardines may be worth 75 points, a can of tomato soup may be worth 50 points, and canned peas may be worth two points. Items that are collected that are not on the list should be worth 25 points. To make the activity even more interesting, 100 points should be awarded to the team that picks up the weirdest, but still edible, canned food item, like canned coconut milk. All items collected should be canned or nonperishable and should be commercially purchased. Divide up the neighborhood into sections and give each team one hour to collect the food. The winning team is the team with the most points. Children should help deliver the food they just collected to a local food bank.

Another fun food drive is a "Trick or Treat Food Drive," which requires adult supervision. As a group, children dress up in costumes and collect canned food items for the food bank instead of candy during the Halloween season. Flyers and posters should be sent out prior to this food drive to explain the nature of this program to the community.

Bigger or Better

Divide the children into smaller teams, with two adult leaders assigned to supervise each team. Give each team a metal thimble and an assignment to go throughout the neighborhood trying to trade and upgrade the thimble to something better to give to a charity thrift store. When the thimble is traded for something better, that item is traded at the next door for something even better. The team has 10 opportunities to trade with 10 different people. At the end of the tenth trade, each team comes back to the center location and is judged on the last item received. All items should be taken to the thrift store at the end of the game. This game teaches children that service can be a lot of fun, in addition to being a rewarding experience.

Service Auction

Children should think of a service that they can perform for another child in the group. Examples include helping with homework, fixing a flat bike tire, taking the family pet for a walk, or making homemade chocolate chip cookies. These service items are sold to the highest bidder and purchased with points, which the children can earn by accomplishing the following tasks during the week:
- Being on time to the program—10 points
- Helping the leaders set up for programs and cleaning up—10 points
- Participating in other activities—25 points
- Completing homework or other assigned projects—25 points

Bake Sale or Car Wash

Bake sales and car washes are fun activities for children. The proceeds earned through these activities can go to the local United Way to help the community. A check from the children should be presented to a United Way official, with the picture and a press release going to the local newspaper.

Clean up a Park or Hiking Trail

For every 10 garbage items picked up in a park or on a trail, the children receive a piece of candy from the leaders. It is important to give each child leather gloves and have them wash their hands after this project. This project is effective not only for the service benefit, but because it teaches the children not to litter in a park or on a hiking trail.

Program #81: Recognition and Praise

Box of Cheers

Fill an empty detergent box with slips of paper, each of which contains one of the following cheers that involve the audience during a campfire program or awards presentation.

Give Me a "B" Cheer—The caller stands in front of the audience and states, "Give me a B," and the audience replies "B." The caller then says, "Give me another B," to which the audience responds with another "B." For a third and final time, the caller asks for a "B." After the audience responds, the caller asks, "What does it spell?" Then he puts his index finger to his lips, and while moving his finger up and down says, "BBBBBBBBBBBBBBBB."

The following are action cheers that require that everyone participates in a uniform action at the same time.

Archery Cheer—This cheer is used to emphasize when a child has done something good and hits the target in his achievement. An adult leads the audience members as they pretend to pull back on an imaginary bow, let go of the imaginary arrow, and say, "Bull's-eye."

The Watermelon Cheer—The audience members pretend they are eating a watermelon by putting their hands to their mouths, slurping the watermelon, and then pretending to spit out the seeds.

Team Cheers

The following are just a few examples of team cheers that rally the team in excitement.

Salsa Cheer—"Salsa, salsa, chips, and dip, we are the ones that are so hip, Rah, Rah Rah!"

Don't Mess Cheer—"Don't mess, don't mess, don't mess with the best cause the best don't rest. Don't fool, don't fool, don't fool with the cool cause the cool don't drool. From the East to the West, our team is the best, go team!"

We Are the Mighty Cheer—"We are the team the mighty, mighty team. Everywhere we go people want to know who we are, so we tell them. Our team is number one!"

Pickles Cheer—"Pickles, pickles, sweet and sour, we are the team with super power. Go Pickles!"

Happy Beads

Give all of the children a leather fob with two inches of plastic lace and 25 heart-shaped red beads. Each time a child receives a compliment from someone else, he gives a bead to that person to hang on his leather fob. This activity teaches the positive benefits of giving and receiving compliments and praise.

Fish Stories

A long time ago, fish mongers discovered as they threw fish to other employees at the fish market that if they made it fun and created an enthusiastic atmosphere, both employees and customers loved being at the fish market. At a quiet time during the day, leaders can ask children to relate a "fish story" in which they saw a child do something nice for another child. The child who did the service is recognized in front of the group by coming forward and picking out fish-shaped candy from a clean goldfish bowl.

Program #82: Journal Writing and Family History

Making Journals

Give each child 25 sheets of paper, 24 inches of plastic lace, and two sheets of cardstock. With a paper punch, have children punch holes in the cardstock for the cover and loop the plastic lace through to make the binding. Children can start writing in their journals, either every day or just after important events. Adults can explain that journals are also great tools to help children process their thoughts, because they write slower than they think, giving them time to sort out their feelings, especially when they are upset or discouraged.

Writing Biographies

In their journals, children can write their life stories and include their hobbies, interests, a list of their best friends, and the names of all of their pets. Children can include their family history going back as many as four generations, as well as a pedigree chart. In addition to their own personal histories, children can include stories about their parents, grandparents, aunts, and uncles. Children can also research how they got their surname, which may give them an idea of what their ancestors did for a living. For example, surnames like, Baker, Potter, Farmer, Smith, and King all came from specific occupations. A last name like Stevenson means "son of Steven." Children will enjoy learning what their last name means.

Chip off the Old Block

Using a five-inch wooden cube, children can smooth out the wood with sandpaper and stain the wood. Once the stain is dry, children can glue a picture of themselves on one side and put pictures of family members on the other sides, including their parents, grandparents, and great-grandparents. Then, they can cover the block with a water-based sealer. Parents should make a copy of the original photographs beforehand.

Family Heritage—Shadow Silhouette

What children look like may be influenced by their family heritage. Making silhouettes may capture those family traits. Start by taping a white sheet of paper on the wall. Each child sits near a lamp that will cast a shadow on the sheet that can be traced by a friend. Then the child places a sheet of black construction paper underneath the white sheet and cuts along the pencil outline, forming a personalized shadow silhouette.

Interviewing a Different Generation

Under adult supervision, have children 10 years of age and older visit a nursing home to interview an older adult about their childhood. Suggested questions that children can ask include the following:

- Where did you live when you were a child?
- What games and activities did you play with your friends?
- Did you have any pets as a child?
- What were your childhood hobbies?
- What did you learn as a child that will help me in growing up?

The benefit of this opportunity is twofold; it provides the chance for an older person to feel respected by a younger person who shows interest in his life, and it gives children the perspective that older adults had similar experiences and issues to the ones that they are facing.

Program #83: Civility and Manners

Etiquette Dinner

Have a progressive dinner during which teenagers as a group go to someone's house for appetizers, soup, and salad, go to another home for the main dish, and still another home for dessert. While in each home, teenagers use their best manners, such as opening the door for others, using the proper fork, and thanking the hosts at each home. Polite conversation with the other guests should take place. The teenagers should offer each dinner host a small gift to express their gratitude.

Dating Game

This activity is designed for teenagers ages 16 and older. All questions that the players ask should be reviewed by an adult leader beforehand. With a divider between one contestant and three dating applicants, a female host asks the male contestants questions to help her decide which young man she wants to date. The answers that each young man gives should entice the young woman to choose him. Questions can be both funny and serious and should help teach the importance of compatibility.

Showing Kindness in a Traffic Jam

Set out one-foot square planks of wood, one for each participant plus one additional board for a free space. Place the boards on the ground in an arch shape. The group is divided into two teams, with equal numbers on both sizes of the free space, which is always in the center of the arch. The two teams are facing each other. By only moving one space forward, not backward, each participant from each side advances forward on one square block at a time. By doing so, the two teams have to trade places by weaving every other participant from each team. For example, the first person from team A (Barry), who is at the front of team A, nearest to the free space, advances to the free space. Next, the first participant from team B (Rachel), who is at the front of team B, steps around Barry and takes his empty spot. Now Barry moves into Rachel's empty spot. The rest of the two teams follow this pattern. The end result should be that team A trades places with team B on the wooden boards. Even with these instructions, the two teams will find that this activity takes time, patience, and planning.

Merging Traffic Lanes

In this game, the children represent cars merging into one lane of traffic. Have a team of six participants place both feet in a large rope circle that is on the ground. The adult leader emphasizes to the team that everyone in the group must fit in the circle and that each participant must have both feet in this circle and all of the other circles throughout the game. Near the rope circle are smaller rope circles. Once the group has fit into one circle, have them choose another one that is smaller than the previous rope circle. As the team moves to the next circle, a leader takes away the circle that they were just in. With each circle, the team has to squeeze in tighter to fit. The last circle is so small that it is impossible for the team of six to stand up and have both feet inside. But then again, the adult leader didn't emphasize that the team had to *stand up*. When the team figures this out, they will lie on the ground and place both of their feet in the circle.

Traffic Light

One person is the "traffic light" in this game. To start the game, the traffic light says "Green light" and the other children, who are "cars" parked 25 feet away, race as fast as they can toward the traffic light. When the traffic light says, "Red light," the cars stop and wait for the green light. The first car to make it to the traffic light becomes the traffic light in the next round.

Do You Love Your Neighbor?

Children sit in chairs in a circle with one less chair than the number of participants. The person left standing is "it" and approaches someone sitting in a chair and asks, "Do you love your neighbor?" If the person replies "Yes," then the people sitting to the right and the left of the person have to exchange places while the person who is "it" tries to take one of the chairs. If the person sitting answers, "No," then he needs to clarify with a comment like, "but I do like people wearing blue pants." All of the participants wearing blue pants exchange places, while the person who is "it" tries to find an empty chair. Whoever is left standing becomes "it" for the next round of this game.

Program #84: Field Trips

Local field trips provide children with knowledge of what is available to do in their neighborhood. In addition to teaching about art and science, field trips can provide opportunities for children to learn about careers and hobbies. Field trips also provide the opportunity for children to gain a deeper appreciation of the products and services provided in their community. Consider the following ideas for fun field trips for children.

Academic Field Trips

- Field science museum
- Zoo
- Aquarium
- Art museum
- Library
- Planetarium
- Aviary
- College or university
- Dinosaur quarry
- State capitol
- City or county buildings
- Theater
- Historic roadside landmark markers
- Auto tour of historic buildings in the community

Field Trips That Explore Careers

During the following field trips, an employee from each business can talk about careers in that industry and provide a tour:

- Cardboard factory
- Candy factory
- Soda pop distribution center
- Farm or dairy
- Bank
- Lawn and garden nursery
- Grocery store
- Police station
- Fire station
- Newspaper agency
- Public park or garden
- Armory
- Art studio
- Retail stores such as a craft, sports, or department store
- Restaurant or bakery
- Golf course or ski resort
- Food bank
- Copy center or printer
- Hotel

Program #85: First Aid and Other Emergencies

Teach CPR and Basic First Aid

Provide children above age 10 with the opportunity to learn CPR and first aid from a certifying agency. During this training, children will practice their emergency skills on mannequins and take a written exam. At the end of the training, children will become certified in CPR and first aid. For teenagers, this training is valuable for summer employment when working as lifeguards or camp counselors.

First Aid Kit

Children of any age should make a first aid kit for their home, backpack, 72-hour kit, or car. With a plastic lightweight toolbox, have children pack the following first aid items: latex gloves, adhesive bandages, antibiotic ointment, eye drops, hydrocortisone cream, moleskin (padding that is placed on the feet to relieve pain from calluses and tender spots), elastic bandage wrap, gauze, athletic tape, scissors, tweezers, a first aid booklet, a list of local emergency numbers, one-way pocket mask, and a cold pack. Instruct children that these items are not toys and that they should not use them without adult supervision.

72-Hour Kit

Children can learn the importance of being prepared during a time of crisis by having a backpack of essential items for survival. Each family should have stored in an accessible location in their home a backpack for each child to take with him at a moment's notice. The following items could be included:

- Bottled water
- Toilet paper
- Small trowel
- Canned food (fruit, beans, tuna fish)
- Can opener
- Trail mix
- Powdered milk
- Mess kit
- Rope
- Pocketknife
- Flashlight
- Spare flashlight batteries
- Whistle
- Emergency blanket
- Water purifier
- Matches
- Towel
- Hand warmers
- Compass
- Solar powered pocket radio

Emergency Cards

Prior to doing this activity, adult leaders should consult local police and emergency-response authorities for approval. Certain communities may have another system that they would rather the group implement.

In this activity, children make and distribute emergency cards to be used during a neighborhood disaster to determine the health and well-being of each household. Three large laminated cards are given to each home with instructions on the back of the cards. The cards should be connected with a key ring and placed in the same location where the 72-hour kits are stored. Each household should place only one card in the front window of their home during the crisis, so emergency workers will know how to respond as they assess the damage in the neighborhood. A green card indicates that everyone in the home is unharmed. A yellow card means that some injuries have taken place but none are severe, and a red card indicates that family members need urgent medical attention.

Amateur Radio Demonstration

Have an amateur radio operator give a workshop on the purpose and function of a radio during an emergency when phone lines are down.

Organize a Neighborhood Crime Watch Program

Children can distribute flyers about organizing a neighborhood watch program, in which adults receive special training and work together to report unusual activities in their neighborhood to local law enforcement agencies. If a child becomes aware of anything that is suspicious in the neighborhood, he is to go to where it is safe and contact a parent, neighbor, or the police department. Through the neighborhood watch program, neighbors are trained to look and listen for the following actions occurring in their neighborhood and contact the police department to investigate these suspicious activities:

- Someone is screaming.
- Property is being taken out of a home when no one is home.
- Someone is being forced into a vehicle.
- A stranger is talking to a neighborhood child.

Program #86: Awareness and Appreciation

Silent Saturday

On a Saturday, have children use only American Sign Language to communicate. Children can carry flashcards of basic signs as well as the alphabet to spell out words. After the activity, ask the children the following two questions: How was their experience with Silent Saturday? How did they gain appreciation for children who cannot hear?

Blind Square

Blindfold the children and have them form a circle holding a long rope. An adult leader instructs the group to form a square, triangle, the state of Utah, and the letter "J," all while blindfolded. Ask the group of children the following two questions: How did the team accomplish the task? What other personal abilities were strengthened when they could not see?

Alignment Games

Divide the group into teams of 15 participants and have each team form a line facing the same direction. While blindfolded and not talking, the team must organize themselves first by their height, then by their birthday, and finally by their shoe size. Ask the team of children the following three questions: What ways were invented by each person to achieve the goal of organizing the team without seeing or talking? How did each participant feel when the team successfully completed this assignment? What challenges in each participant's life are like this assignment?

Wheelchair Appreciation

Children are assigned to perform certain functions in a wheelchair to get an appreciation of children who are in wheelchairs. While sitting in a wheelchair, the children should wash their hands in a bathroom sink and dry them with a bathroom hand dryer. Other tasks can include going through a door, getting a drink from a drinking fountain, and getting help from someone to get up and down stairs. Ask the following two questions of the children who performed these tasks: What was frustrating? What recommendations would the children suggest to others to make them feel more independent while in a wheelchair?

Guide Dog Workshop

Make arrangements for a guide dog trainer to come and discuss the special role that guide dogs have in assisting blind and visually impaired people around obstacles. Have the trainer bring a guide dog and introduce the children to the dog.

Become a Friend

Children should volunteer to be a friend to someone in their school or neighborhood with a special need or who needs a little more acceptance and patience from others. Children who take this opportunity will likely find that they are the one who learned the most when they were a friend to a child with special needs.

Ice Cream Social and Clothespin Game

Invite children with developmental needs as special guests to an ice cream social and play the clothespin game. To play this game, create partnerships between a child and a special guest and give each pair a bag of clothespins with their names written on them. As the group mingles, each partnership gives out clothespins to other partnerships when asked what their names are and what they like to do for fun. The partnership that has collected the most clothespins and is wearing them on their shirts wins the game.

Volunteer at a Special Olympics Event

Children can be timers for races, help with awards, and assist with refreshments at a Special Olympics event.

11

Adult Mentoring

This chapter is designed for adult mentoring settings in which the adult-to-child ratio is reduced so that more opportunities exist for children to learn from adult leadership. Adults have a chance to make a stronger impression when working with smaller groups of children. A minimum of two adult leaders should be with each small group of four to six children. For the protection of the adults and the children, no adult leader should ever be alone with a child.

With certain programs in this chapter (shooting, sports, archery, and canoeing), an adult leader should have certification from a certifying organization. The director of the camp or organization should observe these leaders' skills to ensure these leaders are qualified to run these programs. Both certification and information about qualification should be recorded and on file.

Program #87: Shooting Sports

The age limits provided after each activity name are suggestions only. Different organizations may have other age-limit guidelines. Camps, schools, and other organizations should review their policies concerning age limits prior to setting up this program.

Electronic Target Shooting Set (Ages 4 to 8)

Commercial electronic toy guns and target sets can be purchased at toy and novelty stores for younger children to practice with. This activity is for *target practice only*. Children shoot the plastic gun, which is operated by batteries, toward a plastic log that has sensors in it. The sensors release a button that pushes the plastic cans of beans off the log. The course can be set up indoors or outdoors. Children should be taught by the adult mentors to respect guns and gun safety by always having close adult supervision, and by not pointing guns at people or animals—*even toy guns!*

Setting up the Shooting Range

A roped-off or fenced shooting range must be organized with a bullet trap and a backstop to safely remove lead bullets. The shooting range is led by a qualified and certified shooting range master, who, with vocal range commands, should oversee each round of target practice and provide training on gun safety and proper loading of the gun. Check with local laws and ordinances for approval to operate a shooting range.

While the range is open, a red flag should be flown high enough to be seen from afar and warning signs should be posted. No possible way should exist for people to access the back of the shooting range. Safety goggles and ear protection should be provided for participants and spectators. All equipment for the shooting range must be locked up when the range is closed, in a closet within a lock room. Ammunition is locked in a separate location.

BB Gun (Ages 8 to 12)

Targets can be set up where children can aim and shoot. Adult mentors can work with the children to increase each child's skill and confidence.

Air Rifle (Ages 13 and older)

The adult mentor can assist older children in focusing on pellet grouping, rather than allowing the children to get disappointed if the pellets do not go through the bull's-eye on the target. Grouping occurs when the holes in the target are gathered in a consistent cluster. The tighter the cluster, the more skill the child or teen has in aiming and shooting. The goal should be to get a "quarter grouping," which is a cluster the size of a quarter.

Black Powder Target Shooting (Ages 16 and older)

Qualified and trained adults need to lead participants in loading and shooting a black powder gun. Targets can be empty milk jugs that are hung from a rope in the sectioned-off shooting range.

Program #88: Time Capsule

Memory Bottle

Adults should prepare items that the children will each pack into a small plastic bottle with birdseed. Each child will place multiple items in his memory bottle. The items will remind the children of their experiences with the group programs. The purpose of the birdseed is to conceal all of the items so that children have to twist and spin the bottle to find the different memory items inside. The following items are from many of the programs described earlier in this book and may represent things learned while the group participated in those activities:

- Pencil
- Gold button
- Small globe
- Crayon
- Foam letter
- Plastic insects
- Plastic jewel
- Pasta
- Chili bean
- Plastic animal
- Pencil eraser
- Paper fastener
- Penny
- Paper clip
- Foam number
- Sunflower seeds
- Pipe cleaner
- Seashell
- Craft stick
- Pony beads
- Plastic lace
- Wiggle eyes

Time Capsule

In a metal box that can be locked, children should place items in plastic storage bags to protect them from water damage. Let children decorate the box with paint to make it look futuristic. The following list provides some sample items to consider including:

- Current pictures of each child with his name and age
- A current magazine
- A listing of popular books, music, and movies
- A current newspaper
- An essay by each child about growing up and some of the challenges they are facing
- Pictures of current technology that the children are using, such as digital cameras, CDs, DVDs, MP3s, a laptop computer, and printouts from the Internet
- A description from children of what they want to be when they grow up
- A list of predictions made about future world affairs and popular culture made by each child
- Illustrations of futuristic tools yet invented to reduce household chores

Time Capsule Groundbreaking Ceremony

Paint several shovels with gold spray paint and have children conduct the groundbreaking ceremony. Have a keynote speaker and serve refreshments. Place a plaque near the time capsule indicating when to open it. Children then dig a hole in the ground, line the hole with a plastic storage container to place the metal box in, seal the plastic container with a lid, and cover the hole with dirt. Invite the local media to the groundbreaking ceremony or provide pictures and a press release for the local newspaper.

Program #89: Archery

A roped-off or fenced archery range should be prepared. A qualified and certified archery range master must lead each round, with vocal range commands ensuring that the bows are strung properly and that the correct arrows are used with the different types of bows. The archery range master will determine the distance of the targets based on the equipment used and the age and ability of the participants. Check with local laws and ordinances for approval to operate an archery range. While the range is open, a red flag should be flown high enough to be seen from afar and warning signs should be posted. No possible way should exist for people to access the back of the archery range. Arrow stop(s) and backdrops should be used. Finger tabs and armguards should be available to avoid discomfort. All equipment must be locked up when the range is closed.

Recurve Bow

For most children under 16 years old, a recurve bow will be the best fit. Adult mentors can assist each child with putting the arrow on the bow and provide encouragement. A flu-flu cedar arrow, which has a large rubber blunt tip and a fletching design that is specifically created to allow the arrow only to travel a short distance, is the perfect arrow for small children between the ages of six and nine. For older children, target arrows can be used. Robin Hood or Joan of Arc awards should be awarded.

Action Archery

With the blunt-tip flu-flu arrows and recurve bows, children can aim at other items besides the traditional target. In action archery, children aim at items that move when struck with arrows, such a weather vein, bells, a sheet of plywood with small flaps on hinges that open and close, a stack of empty tin cans, or a stuffed animal suspended from a rope. The archery range master needs to assess the child's strength to determine the distance from the target.

3-D Archery Course

In a roped-off area, participants over the age of 12 can shoot at three-dimensional foam targets shaped like deer, bears, turkeys, or raccoons that are hidden in the trees, using target arrows and recurve bows. The archery range master must ensure that the entire area is secure, so that no one accidentally comes into the course. Make sure the area is roped off, with a red flag that is visible.

Compound Bow

For teenage participants ages 16 and older, a compound bow is a way to add speed and precision to target practice. Competition between participants can be organized by the archery range master so that each participant is given five practice arrows for the first round and five arrows for the tournament. Counting from the center ring outward, points are awarded depending on where the arrow hits on the target.

Program #90: Slingshots

Slingshot Range (Ages 12 and older)

To begin, rope or fence off a slingshot range with a tarp backdrop to catch the quarter-inch steel hunting shot. A qualified and trained adult must lead each round of slingshot shooting with vocal range commands and ensure that the slingshots are in good condition and that everyone wears eye protection. Check with local laws and ordinances for approval to operate a slingshot range. Instruct children never to draw bands back to their eyes, because serious injuries could occur. While the range is open, a red flag should be flown high enough to be seen from afar and warning signs should be posted. No possible way should exist for people to access the back of the slingshot

range. Adult mentors can help the children develop confidence by offering praise as they acquire this new skill. If a child is struggling, mentors should be there to help them succeed. All equipment must be locked up when the range is closed.

Target Competition

Children can compete by using scoring paper targets. The Huck Finn Award can be given to the participant with the highest score.

Balloon Course

Instead of paper targets, adults can run a string across with several four-inch dart balloons attached. Water balloons are also effective targets, because they explode when hit. Balloons should only be half-filled with water so that they don't get too heavy.

Candy Clean Up

Children can be rewarded with a piece of candy for every five steel balls that they pick up that the tarp didn't hold. This activity teaches children to be considerate of the environment and is an effective way to gather the ammo, which is reusable. For safety reasons, make sure the course is completely put away before children are allowed to start picking items up off the ground.

Program #91: Storytelling Festival

Set up large tents for adult storytellers and small tents for read-a-thons (which are covered later in this program) and children's storytelling activities. Divide the children into smaller groups so that the storytellers can interact one-on-one with each child.

Storytellers

Libraries, college theater departments, and local storytelling clubs are great resources when reserving storytellers. Teams of children should rotate from one location to another, while each storyteller stays in the same tent for the whole day. Each presentation should be approximately 30 minutes long so that children hear a sample of different types of stories or songs over the course of the day. Storytellers should submit story topics indicating what type of story they will be telling so that adult leaders can separate teams by the type of story presented for each session. By the end of the festival, all teams should have attended each storyteller's session.

Spinning a Yarn

Long ago, when ships were out to sea, seamen would spend rainy days under shelter spinning and twisting yarns of old rope to be used for other jobs. While performing this mundane task, they would tell stories. Spinning a yarn became an expression meaning to stretch the truth like the yarn of rope while telling a story. When participating in this activity, children sit on the ground in a circle. The leader gives one child a roll of yarn to start spinning into a ball while starting a story. After a few minutes, this child gives the yarn to someone else in the circle, who picks up the story where the first person left off and continues wrapping the yarn into a ball. All the children in the circle should participate in the telling of this story and spinning the yarn. At the end of this activity, children should have a great story that they all told together—and one big ball of yarn.

Tall-Tale Fish Contest

In addition to formal adult storytellers, one session should be devoted to a contest in which children compete before a panel of judges in telling the most creative fish story. The winner of this competition should receive a storytelling trophy.

To Start a Story

Children can be coached by adult leaders on storytelling techniques. One technique is to start a story that will capture the audience's imagination right from the beginning. The storyteller jumps in from the start with the date, time, and place to set the scene of the story. For example: "It was a dark and stormy night, Friday the thirteenth, in the funhouse of the amusement park, when. . . ."

Read-a-Thon

In a smaller tent full of pillows and books, children participate in a read-a-ton for two hours, during which they are awarded bookmarks as prizes when they either read 20 picture books or 40 pages in a chapter book.

Program #92: Fishing

Time Well Spent

The excitement and thrill of fishing is only enhanced by the opportunity for children to talk and interact with adults. Adult leaders spend so much time in other programs planning, implementing, and supervising children that little time is spent in relaxed conversation between adult and child. This opportunity for mentoring is very precious.

Hunting for Bait

Commercial bait can be purchased, but most children think that hunting for worms is half the fun of fishing. At night, with an empty soup can and flashlight, adults and children can flip over rocks and dig in the earth for worms. Place moist dirt in the empty can before placing the worms in. Extra bait can be sold either at a curbside stand or to a tackle and bait shop.

Practice Casting

Children can practice their casting skills by casting into a bucket of water with a weight on their line. The advantage of practicing in an open area, such as a lawn or parking lot, is that children can cast without worrying about tangling their line in overhanging trees. When children increase their skills, they are ready for the river or lake.

Bamboo Pole

Go back in time by having children make their own fishing poles with string, a hook, and a bamboo pole, and then send them fishing. Don't forget to give each child a beachcomber hat and a can of worms.

Fly Fishing

Have an adult lead a workshop in tying flies and give each child a fishing fly for his tackle box. Children can also practice casting using the different techniques used in fly fishing.

Department of Fish and Game

Invite an employee of the local fish and game department to talk to children about managing fish hatcheries, preventing the spread of harmful diseases among fish, and fishing opportunities in the area.

Program #93: Rope Activities

Whipping, Fusing, and Dipping Rope Ends

The purpose of whipping a rope is to wrap string around an end of a piece of rope to prevent it from fraying. To start, children can take a string and place it up against an end of the rope. Then, they make a large loop the size of their hand with one end of the string. Then, children thread the other end of the string through the loop and begin wrapping that end around the rope four times. To secure the string to the rope, children should pull the string end through the four wrapped sections and cut off both ends of the string. With nylon or plastic rope that has become frayed, children can fuse the rope by burning the frayed ends together over a candle, under close adult supervision. Dipping synthetic rope into paint will also bind the ends of the rope.

Magic Rope

Tie a loop on both ends of the rope and then put one on each wrist of a child. Another child's rope is crossed under the first child's rope, with both ends looped around the second child's wrist. Have the children try to undo the rope tangle without cutting it or taking it off their wrists. The solution is to pull one person's loop under and around the other person's rope and wrist and slip that person's hand through while the rope stays on the wrists of both children.

Knots

Teach children the following knots and then have a team relay in which each child ties a different knot—figure eight, clove hitch, tautline, two half hitches, bowline, timber hitch, square knot, sheet bend, and slipknot. Adult leaders may want to give each child two different colors of rope when teaching knots. It is also a good idea to glue sample knots onto a sheet of plywood so that children can refer to the three-dimensional example as they are learning each knot.

Lashings

Three types of lashings that children can learn are the square, diagonal, and shear. The square lashing is started with a clove hitch on the vertical log underneath the horizontal log. Then, wrap the rope around both ends of the intersection where the logs meet with each layer of rope on the outside of the previous section. After three wrapping turns, make two frapping turns, which involves running the rope over the wrapping turns, placing rope over rope, and tying it off with a clove hitch. With the diagonal hitch, children make a timber hitch and three turns around the logs where the rope lays side by side. In the other diagonal direction, they make three more turns crosswise and pull the rope tight. Apply two turns of frapping between the logs and the diagonal lashings, tying off the lashings with a clove hitch. The third lashing is the shear lashing. Children begin by laying two logs side by side, tying a clove hitch on one log. Wrap the log with eight turns of rope and then two complete frapping turns between the logs onto the eight turns of rope and finish with a clove hitch.

SQUARE LASHING

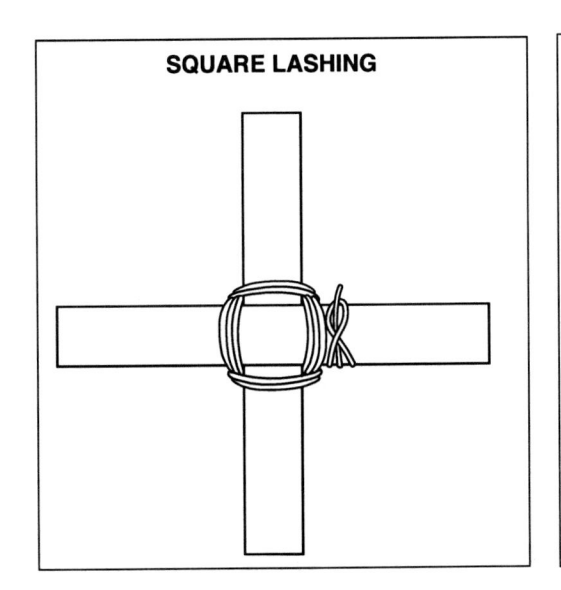

DIAGONAL LASHING

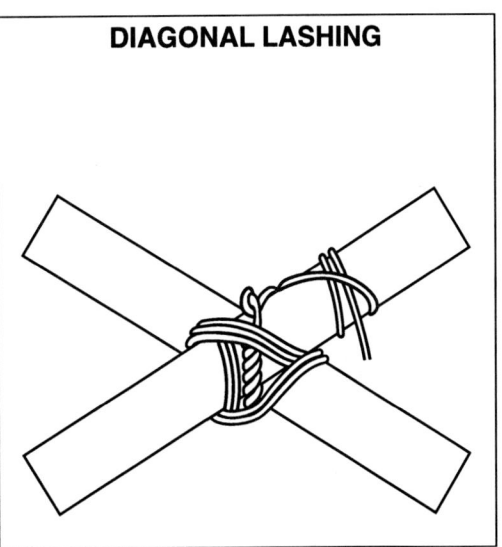

SHEER LASHING

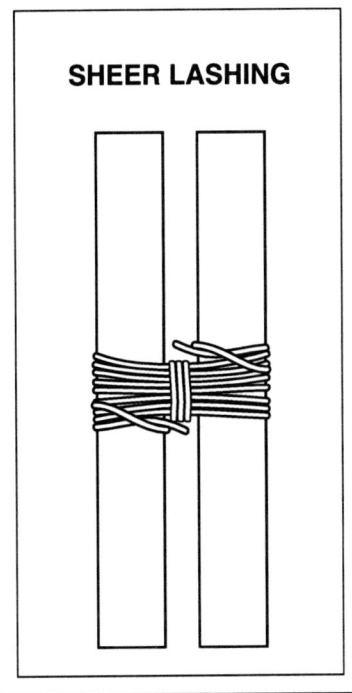

Rope and Golf Ball Toss

To prepare for this activity, set up a PVC-pipe rack with three different three-quarter-inch pipes as the crossbars. The top crossbar is connected to a pair of three-quarter-inch elbows. The other two crossbars are connected to a vertical stand. The six pieces of three-quarter-inch pipe that make up the vertical stand are one foot long and are connected with three-quarter-inch "T" fittings. On the base of the stand are two 15-inch pipes that are connected to a three-quarter-inch "T" fitting.

To attach the golf balls, adults drill a hole in the ball, and run rope through each ball, tying off the ends. Then, adults add epoxy glue to keep the rope secure. The length of the rope between the balls is 15 inches.

To play rope and golf ball toss, children throw the golf balls that are connected to each other with rope. The three crossbeams are each worth different point values. Children stand six feet away and try to earn points by wrapping the roped balls around the beams. The child with the most points wins the activity.

Program #94: Firesides

Campfire Chats

Around a nighttime campfire, adults can have formal programs in which college professors or forest rangers talk about astronomy, local folklore, nocturnal animals in the area, and Native American or pioneer stories. Local sports athletes can be invited to speak about setting goals.

Avoiding Illegal Drugs

A police officer or medical official can address the importance of avoiding illegal drugs and explain the consequences of taking drugs from both a legal and safety perspective. Children should role play situations that they may find themselves in at school and discuss how to confront each situation by saying no and walking away. Adult mentors can coach and advise children as they role play, and should provide alternative ways to avoid peer pressure.

Inspirational Speaker

Inspirational topics that adult presenters can speak on include poetry, patriotism, self-worth, and service to others. Adults can also provide examples of triumph in which individuals overcame difficulties through a positive attitude and determination.

Warm Fuzzy Exchange

In a campfire setting, give each child a small craft pom-pom and have them give a "warm fuzzy" to someone else while saying something nice about that person. Adult mentors should make sure that everyone in the group is included in the activity and that no one is left out.

The Sounds of the Night

Adult mentors can give a thought-provoking talk on success and happiness, and then allow children time to reflect on the message. In a nighttime campfire setting, children can listen to the sounds of the night as they ponder the remarks of the speaker. Allow children time to write down in their journals the impressions they felt during this experience. In an indoor setting, children can listen to soft classical music as they write their feelings down in their journal.

Serving Refreshments

Finish off the fireside activity with refreshments. This time is also an opportunity for children to visit with each other and with adult mentors and to process the fireside message.

Program #95: Canoeing

A certified lifeguard or waterfront director who has specialized training and certification in small watercraft should supervise canoeing activities with adults and children. Each participant should demonstrate his swimming skills, as well as his boarding and debarking skills, either on a dock or on the shore prior to the canoeing activity. All equipment must be locked up when the waterfront is closed. Refer to Chapter 7, Program #60 for recommendations on determining children's swimming abilities.

Basic Canoeing Skills

Children and their adult mentors should learn the following basic strokes before starting their canoe activity: the forward stroke, the stern steering stroke for the person at the stern of the canoe, the "J" stroke, and the cross draw stroke for the person at the bow of the canoe. Both adults and children should wear personal floatation devices, and a bailing bucket and a rescue bag should be attached inside the canoe.

Swamping the Canoe in Shallow Water

If the canoe fills with water and starts to sink, it can still be paddled to shore by using both ends of the paddle to move forward. Another alternate for a swamped canoe is to perform a canoe-over-canoe rescue, or "T" rescue, with the help of another canoe. To perform this technique, the rescue canoe approaches the capsized canoe. While the people in the water hold the rescue canoe steady, the capsized canoe is swung around at a right angle to the rescue canoe. The capsized canoe is tipped on its side to let the water drain out. While still on its side, the canoe is raised over the rescue canoe so that it lays bottom-up on the rescue canoe. The capsized canoe is then rolled back over to its proper position on the rescue canoe's gunwales, where it can be eased back into the water and the individuals in the water can return to their canoe. The people in the rescue canoe can hold the canoe steady to ease the reentry of the people in the water.

Reentry

For adults, the following instructions are given concerning the arm-across reentry, which is the easiest way to get into the canoe from deep water. This method involves reaching to the other side of the canoe with one hand, bracing the other arm to the closer side, and steadying the canoe as you pull yourself into the canoe. For children, flopping over into the canoe is easier. This technique involves the child leaning over the gunwale of the canoe and flopping into the canoe headfirst while ducking his head down and tucking his legs under his body. The child should roll onto his back as he lands in the bottom of the canoe.

Canoeing Skill Courses

Set up a course with empty milk jugs that are tied to anchors. Six empty milk jugs float in a straight line with 20 feet separating them. The canoe can weave in and out of the course. Another course that can be built with empty milk jugs is a 60-foot triangle-shaped course. The canoe can also maneuver in a circle around one floating milk jug.

Paddling to the Beat of a Drum

As part of appreciating Native-American culture, have the child and the adult mentor paddle to the beat of a drum as another child dressed in a Native-American headdress beats a drum on the shore.

Bird Watching

When canoeing quietly and slowly on a pond or lake, many opportunities exist to observe birds and other wildlife up close without startling them away. A pocket-sized bird guide can be carried to identify the various birds. Children will increase their appreciation of nature and have a chance to talk with their adult mentors as they canoe quietly over the still water.

Programs #96: Roundtable Discussions

For children 11 years or older, roundtable discussions are informal ways to have adult presenters interact with participants. Small groups sit around a table while an adult presenter leads the discussion. Several discussion groups can be going on at the same time, with a half-hour session taking place before each group moves to another table.

Book Roundtable Discussion

At each table, a librarian, teacher, or older young adult leads a discussion on different new books so that participants learn about different books to read. A special table in the room can be devoted to a certain book that all of the participants have read. They should have an in-depth discussion of the book's story and characters.

Life Skills Roundtable Discussion

Adult mentors can teach different life skills at each table, such as ironing, sewing, cooking, doing the laundry, shopping, basic home repair, changing the oil in a car, or gardening.

Financial and Time-Management Roundtable Discussion

For young adults preparing for college and living on their own, invite a local branch manager of a bank to talk about savings and avoiding excessive debt. Other roundtable discussions can include living on a budget, money-saving tips for grocery shopping, balancing a checkbook, buying a car, or time management.

Summer Job Fair

Invite summer camps, city recreation departments, golf courses, and other summer-based companies to set up booths for the youth group to promote summer employment.

School Recruitment Fair

Invite several colleges and universities, military recruiters, and scholarship counselors to a recruitment fair where young adults have a chance to gather information concerning their future educational opportunities.

Program #97: Hobby Night

Organize a hobby night during which children exhibit their hobbies at booths located throughout the room. Examples of hobby presentations include bringing the family pet, displaying a painting, and playing a musical instrument. A craft fair can also be included in the event during which items such as knitting, quilts, homegrown fruits and vegetables, and woodworking projects can be sold at booths.

Commercial Exhibitors and Workshops

Invite specialty retail stores to provide workshops for a nominal registration fee. The following list presents suggested workshops:

- A craft store can run a workshop on candle making.
- A fabric store could provide a workshop on making neckties or tying fleece blankets.
- An outdoor camping store might teach about water-purification filters for backpacking.
- A restaurant supply store could teach a class on cake decorating.
- A hobby store can run a remote-control racecars demonstration.
- A bookstore can provide the "book of the month" to participants ahead of time and hold a book club meeting.
- A hardware store can provide building materials and tools to make wooden birdhouses.

Youth Community Clubs

Invite community clubs to recruit new members. Community clubs may include the following:

- Amateur Radio Club
- American Sign Language Club
- Chinese Cooking Club
- Cultural Club
- Fencing Club
- Flower Arrangement Club
- Fly Fishing Club
- Genealogy Club
- Middle Ages Club
- Mountain Biking Club
- Quilting Club
- Rock Collecting Club
- Rock Climbing Club
- Running Club
- Service Club
- Science Fiction Club
- Social Dance Club

Board Game Tournament

Divide the group into smaller teams to play board games. The winner of each board game plays other winners until an overall winner is crowned for the entire tournament.

Program #98: Postcard Road Rally

Preparation

Divide the group into teams of four participants, each with an adult driver and another adult leader. Each team needs a digital camera for the road rally and a list of pictures to acquire during the journey. A central location of where the groups are to meet and at what time they should return should be communicated prior to the trip. The group organizers should make arrangements for a projector, a screen, and several laptop computers to be set up prior to all of the groups returning back to the central location.

The Objective

The objective of this activity is to create a postcard slideshow of the group at different locations throughout the community to prove that the group was actually at the location. Everyone in the group, except the designated photographer, should be in every picture.

Safety

All traffic laws should be obeyed and all participants should wear seatbelts as they travel. Respect to other people and property should be shown at all times during this activity.

The List of Photo Opportunities

The list of photographs should be organized so that the same items are on all of the lists, but the items should be listed in a different order to prevent groups from arriving at the same location at the same time. The list of pictures can also be general enough that groups can pick from several locations in the community, such as a picture of the team shaking hands with a used car salesman. The following list presents ideas of places and people for a postcard road rally:

- Sitting in swings in a park
- Holding a jar of pickles at a grocery store (get permission from the store manager first)
- Reading a picture book at a library
- Climbing stairs in an indoor stairwell
- Picking up litter off the ground
- Sitting down in front of a football field
- Getting a drink from an outdoor drinking fountain
- Standing by a green car in a parking lot

- Holding a volleyball
- Standing by a sign that has the letter "M"
- Forming a circle around a historical marker or statue
- Making a smiley face with everyone's shoes in front of a pine tree
- Sitting on cement steps
- Standing on or near a bridge
- Sitting in a vehicle with each person wearing a seatbelt
- Standing by flowers
- Standing by a person in a blue hat

Slideshow

Once every team returns to the central location, it will take a few minutes to download each team's pictures onto the computer. During this time refreshments can be served to the group. All teams should watch the slideshow of each team's journey. A panel of judges scores each team's slideshow and chooses a winner based upon originality and creativity. A bag of mini-candy bars should be awarded to each team for their participation.

Program #99: Start a Collection Hobby

Children should be encouraged to start a collection that they can bring to a hobby night and display. Collections can include just about anything that is safe and that the child's parents will allow him to keep in their house. Consider the following examples of fun hobby collections:

- Birthday cards
- Bookmarks
- Bouncy balls
- Books or magazines
- Bumper stickers
- Business cards
- Candy dispensers
- Camp or program patches
- Christmas tree ornaments
- Coins
- Costumes
- Comic books
- Dolls
- Frisbees
- Die-cast metal cars
- Halloween masks
- Hats
- Lapel pins
- Key chains
- Magnets
- Matchbooks (containing no matches)
- Movie ticket stubs
- Mugs
- Music boxes
- Pens and pencils
- Pocketknives
- Poems or stories
- Postage stamps
- Postcards
- Rocks and fossils
- Salt and pepper shakers
- Seashells
- Silver spoons
- Small glass or ceramic figurines
- Snow globes
- Soda bottles or bottle caps
- Sports or movie cards
- Sports pennants
- State or country flags
- Sunday newspaper comics
- Themed collectible items such as cows, chickens, or sunflowers
- Thimbles
- Toy action figures
- Toy animals (either plastic or stuffed animals)
- Toys from restaurant children's meals
- Yo-yos

Program #100: Leadership Training Taught by Children

Older children can prepare a leadership-training workshop. The advantage of children teaching their peers is that those that prepare lessons enhance their own knowledge of a leadership principle by researching the topic. The level of respect given by children to the child instructor also increases because children gain a deeper appreciation of what it feels like to stand in front of others trying to teach. Each workshop should be 20 minutes long with a 10 minute activity. Adult mentors still play an important role in coaching the child instructors as they prepare their lessons.

Leadership Versus Management

A child teaches the difference between managing and leading. To illustrate the difference, the team of children is asked to form a straight line and hold a jump rope. A child who is chosen then tries to move the group by gently pushing the jump rope five feet. This exercise represents how less effective it is to "push" people to accomplish tasks. Then the same child, who is now called a "leader," gently pulls the rope five feet to represent leading people to accomplishing tasks. The child instructor then teaches how to lead a group of people to accomplish assignments.

Vision and Planning

A child presents this section about the importance of establishing a vision and a goal of what the team wants to accomplish. The team can write a mission statement of what their objective is and study other mission statements from companies and organizations. To teach this concept, the child instructor can have the group create a chain link fence design with colorful plastic cups. The type of design is determined by the team members, who collaborate on a vision of what the design should look like and what colors to use. Then the team goes to work and inserts the cups into the holes of the fence in a certain pattern.

Delegating

A child leads a discussion about delegating tasks to others to get the job done. One person is selected to be the leader of the team and is given 10 air-filled balloons that he has to keep floating in the air at the same time without letting them touch the ground. After a few minutes of trying to accomplish this task, the leader then delegates to 10 other children on the team. Each child takes one of the balloons and only keeps that balloon from hitting the ground. The child instructor can point out the challenge of trying to balance 10 balloons in the air and the advantage of allowing more people to help with the task.

Time Management

The child giving this workshop can make a list of all of the things that a typical child might do in a given day, such as get ready for school, pack a lunch, catch the bus, attend school, practice the piano, play video games, play with friends, baby-sit a little brother, complete homework assignments, watch television, mow the lawn, play outside, and do the dinner dishes. To help children organize their time so that they accomplish the tasks assigned by others as well as find time to do fun activities of their choosing, they should make a list of the items that they have to do and want to do. To teach children about prioritizing, the child instructor can fill a gallon-sized plastic container to the top with sand and then try to make two baseballs fit inside the container. The sand represents all the things that a child wants to do, like play video games, play outside with friends, and watch TV. The two baseballs represent the things the child must do, like homework, doing the dinner dishes, and practicing the piano. If the child waits until the end to add the baseballs, no room is left. A child who starts doing homework at 9:00 p.m. after watching TV and playing video games all afternoon is in this situation. The secret to getting everything accomplished is making a list of things to do and prioritize the items that should be done first—put the baseballs in the container first and then add the sand.

Teamwork

The child who teaches the leadership principle of teamwork can give examples of sports teams who worked together to win an important game and of the coaches who motivated the team to succeed through teamwork. To further clarify this concept, the child instructor divides the group into two teams and gives each team a 50-piece puzzle to be completed by everyone on the team. Prior to the workshop, the contents of each puzzle box should be divided in half, so that half of each puzzle is mixed in with the other puzzle's pieces. When children realize that the two teams are not competing with each other, but instead represent a larger team, they will quickly start sharing puzzle pieces so both smaller teams can complete the assignment.

Program #101: Prevention Activities and Training Drills to Avoid Becoming Lost

Adults should be concerned for each child's safety more than the recreational program being provided. Adult mentors need to have strong stewardship for each child in their care and take every precaution necessary to prevent a child from becoming lost. Written procedures preventing and dealing with lost children should be available for all adult leaders before starting any program.

Prevention

This program is designed to prevent children from being lost in the outdoors. It gives leaders and children the tools, resources, and confidence so that if anyone becomes separated from the group, he will keep a "cool head" until he is reunited with the group.

Keeping Track of Young Children

When walking with a group of young children under the age of six, adults should carry a long plastic jump rope that they call a "train." Each child pretends that he is a train car and holds onto the rope. The front leader is the "engine" and the last leader holding onto the rope is the "caboose." The train travels as slow as the slowest child, so no one trips or gets stepped on. A piece of tape should be attached to the back of each child with his name on it. One leader does a routine head-count while referring to the list of children for whom he is responsible. Other children may be in the area that are not in the group, so referring to the list is very important.

Hiking With Children

As children are hiking, an easy way for leaders to keep track of each child is by assigning each child a number. Every so often, the leaders conduct a "count-off" drill in which the children count off their numbers. One leader should hike in front of the group and another should be behind the group with little or no gaps in the middle. A game can be made out of the following safety rules in which fruit snacks are awarded for answers given concerning hiking safety.

- Never go anywhere alone—stay together
- Never take shortcuts—stay on the trail
- Wear long pants and hiking boots
- Stay on the trail to avoid coming in contact with snakes and poisonous plants
- Do not run down the trails

Communication

As trips are planned, cell phones or two-way radios should be packed.

Preparing for the Activity

During a camping outing in the outdoors, children should carry with them a small backpack that contains extra water, some food, a whistle, a compass, matches, a map of the area, a small mirror in a plastic container, a rain poncho, a pocketknife, an emergency blanket, and a flashlight. Rules should be communicated about the buddy system. A role-playing activity should be organized in which each child is informed of what to do if he becomes separated from the group. The following are suggested basic instructions that can be written on a small card and carried with each child, in case they become separated from the group:

- Stop walking, sit down, and wait to be found. Try to become visible as soon as possible without traveling too far from where you discovered that you were lost. The common instinct when lost is to wander around aimlessly, making matters worse.

- Use a whistle instead of yelling. Blow three times every few minutes to indicate that you are in distress. In the daytime, reflect the sunlight off of the mirror. At nighttime, shine the flashlight as a way to signal your location every 20 minutes.

- Don't panic. Keep your mind focused on things other than being lost. Sing camp songs to pass the time or spend time reviewing your map and compass to gain an understanding of where you are. You still need to wait to be found!
- Answer any shouts and signals you hear.
- Be careful of strangers who want to take you somewhere. It is best to stay in the same location where you were lost. If a stranger wants to help, he can notify the authorities of your location so your group can find you. Rangers, search and rescue personnel, and sheriff departments will introduce themselves to you and show you identification.
- Don't drink the natural water.
- Sit in the shade and conserve energy. Ration out your food and water.
- If the weather is bad, build a shelter of boughs or sticks or go under a large pine tree, use your emergency blanket and rain poncho to stay warm and dry.

About the Author

Jared R. Knight is the manager of programs for more than 5,000 children each year at the BYU Aspen Grove Family Camp, where he has been since 1996. He is also the president of the Southwest Section of the American Camp Association, where he is also a Standards Visitor.

Knight started serving children as a missionary for the Church of Jesus Christ of Latter-day Saints in Canada, where he volunteered for the Boys and Girls Club. He received a bachelor of science degree in recreation management and youth leadership and a master's degree in public administration from Brigham Young University. Knight has also served as the director of development for United Way of Utah County, and as a camp director for the Boy Scouts of America. He has also been on several boards of directors for community-based organizations focusing on the health, recreation, and education of children.

He and his wife, LaDonna, live in Utah with their three children, Rachel, Alex, and Emerson.